HIDDEN

in

PLAIN SIGHT

HIDDEN
in
PLAIN SIGHT

How Men's Fears of Women Shape Their Intimate Relationships

Avrum G. Weiss, Ph.D.

Foreword by James M. O'Neil, Ph.D.

Lasting Impact Press

Pontiac, IL

Hidden in Plain Sight: How Men's Fears of Women Shape Their Intimate Relationships

Publisher: Lasting Impact Press, an imprint of Connection Victory Publishing Company P.O. Box 563, Pontiac, IL61764-0563

For information regarding licensing this content, or to order in bulk, please write to the publisher: inforequest@connectionvictory.com

Author: Avrum G. Weiss, Ph.D.

Foreword Author: James M. O'Neil, Ph.D

Developmental Editor: L. Michelle Tullier, Ph.D.

Editor: Lisa M. Blacker

Associate Editor: E.G. Regan

Photo of Author: Julia Curran Photography

Publisher's Cataloging-in-Publication Data

Names: Weiss, Avrum G., 1953-.
Title: Hidden in plain sight : how men's fears of women shape their intimate relationships / Avrum G. Weiss, Ph.D. ; foreword by James M. O'Neil, Ph.D.
Description: Pontiac, IL : Connection Victory Publishing, 2021. | Summary: Popular non-fiction book explores relationships and the hidden internal world of men. Presents many scenarios with prescriptive content and guidance woven throughout.
Identifiers: LCCN 2021947890 | ISBN 9781643810454 (pbk.) | ISBN 9781643810386 (KDP pbk.) | ISBN 9781643810447 (IngramSpark pbk.) | ISBN 9781643810393 (Amazon ebook) | ISBN 9781643810409 (epub) | ISBN 9781643810416 (PDF)
Subjects: LCSH: Man-woman relationships -- Psychology. | Masculinity. | Men -- Conduct of life. | Men -- Identity. | Men's studies. | Sex role. | BISAC: FAMILY & RELATIONSHIPS / Marriage & Long-Term Relationships. | SELF-HELP / Gender & Sexuality. | SOCIAL SCIENCE / Men's Studies.
Classification: LCC HQ1088.W45 2021 | DDC 305.31 W4--dc23
LC record available at https://lccn.loc.gov/2021947890

Dedication

To my wife Michelle, who has helped me love a woman with less fear.

To the hundreds of men over the decades who have honored me by talking courageously and openly about their fears. You are my primary teachers.

To the faculty of the graduate psychology department of the University of West Georgia who taught me a way of listening to and understanding lived experience that has sustained me for forty-five years.

To my dearest friend Bob Carrere, with whom I have shared the pleasure of learning for forty-five years.

To Debbara Dingman, Ph.D., my colleague and co-therapist for so long that I've lost track of where her ideas leave off and mine begin.

To Dick Bathrick, who challenged my thinking and pushed me to consider how this work might be misinterpreted in harmful ways.

To Michelle Tullier, Jim O'Neil, Judith Jordan, and Murray Scher, and Carrie Phillips who read the manuscript and gave me invaluable feedback.

Advanced Praise for Hidden in Plain Sight

"Dr. Avrum Weiss' book *Hidden in Plain Sight* beautifully weaves together the personal and collective stories of fearful men and women, bringing us closer to understanding the real complexity of male-female relationships—not a small feat! Dr. Weiss' wisdom and perspective illuminate the influence of power and privilege on gender. His empathy for men's struggles is palpable and kind, as is his ability to locate the source of pain: not in men or women but in patriarchy itself.

This is a courageous book that can help all of us move beyond polarizing gender stereotypes. Radical empathy offers the possibility of real change; Dr. Weiss' balanced and deep empathy shows us the way out of the isolation of silence and how, together, we can gather skills and create hope, bringing about personal and social wellbeing. If we are to change the world, we must first reduce the fear that hustles us toward isolation and silence. *Hidden in Plain Sight* opens the way for fresh and frank discussions between women and men."

~~ Judith V Jordan. Ph.D.
Assistant Professor of Psychiatry, Harvard Medical School,
Author of Relational-Cultural Therapy

"This book is needed now more than ever. I want to buy it for everyone I know. When men go silent, all of us lose something vital. To live with, love, raise, and work with boys and men, it is imperative that we understand the world as men live in it. Dr. Weiss has truly written a new psychology of men."

~~ Carrie Phillips, LISW

"I had honestly never in my life heard men talk this way, to articulate that the women in their lives were so profoundly important to them that they were constantly terrified we'd leave them—a threat I had often made in my rages, semi-seriously at times, assuming it had no impact."

~~ Anonymous female participant of Dr. Weiss'
"Men's Fears of Women" workshop.

"In this thought-provoking book, Dr. Weiss blends decades of clinical experience and brutally honest personal accounts to illustrate the underlying emotional roadblocks that interfere with men's relationships with women. He explores attachment and separation in parent-child relationships and the gender role socialization process that men experience in society at large. The reader is left with a blueprint for understanding conflicts in relationships and for making the course corrections that can lead to more authentic and fulfilling relationships. I will incorporate these insights into my future clinical work with couples."

~~ Bill DeFranc, Ph.D.
Licensed Psychologist, University of Massachusetts, Boston

"Although centered on relational fears of straight men, *Hidden in Plain Sight* will enrich gay men's understanding of fears that might exist in any intimate pair. More importantly, it might help you understand a possibly universal conflict of gay youths. As a child I thought I was an outsider looking into the world of masculinity. I felt unsettled at not being fully male and thought that straight kids really knew what I did not: how to be a boy and ultimately a man. But I now see how straight guys were just as lost as I was in feeling not masculine enough. It was all a false-self performance that left no one satisfied or safe. So I only imagined that I was an outsider. I was an outsider among outsiders!"

~~ Robert Carrere, Ph.D., ABPP
Psychoanalyst/Clinical Psychologist

Table of Contents

Foreword

Men's fears of women—a phenomenon "hidden in plain sight"—is a pervasive reality that negatively affects men's lives. When any psychological phenomenon goes unnamed and unexamined, or is known but denied, we are more vulnerable to its negative effects. That is why *Hidden in Plain Sight: How Men's Fears of Women Shape Their Intimate Relationships* is an important book. Dr. Avrum Weiss, a psychologist in private practice for more than thirty-five years, reveals how men's fears of women and femininity result in conscious and unconscious sexism and gender role conflict and ultimately have a negative impact on men, on women, and on their relationships.

Weiss argues that men experience seven fears of women, including: fear of being dominated and controlled; fear of entrapment; fear of failure to protect and provide; fear of women's emotions; fear of being inadequate; fear of being abandoned; and fear of being feminine. He provides justification for these fears of women using past theory, research, and his own extensive clinical experience. And, he explains how awareness of these fears and adopting new ways of communicating through them can alleviate serious problems that men, women, and couples often face.

Groundbreaking Work

Hidden in Plain Sight makes a significant contribution to the psychology of men and the field of men's studies. Having researched, written about, and taught in the areas of men and masculinity, gender role conflict, psychology of men and women, and violence and victimization for over four decades, I see this book as breaking significant new ground. The fear of women and femininity were political and interpersonal issues that shaped the earliest days of the profession of psychology. So, conceptually, the fear of women is not new; it has a scattered and fragmented history in the psychological literature. What is new is Weiss' bold and direct handling of the role that patriarchal sexism plays in men's psychological problems and the fear of women. These problems are not caused by women but by a patriarchal system that seeks to control others and make profits based on destructive stereotypes that harm others. It is refreshing to see such a direct indictment of the patriarchy as the cause of so much suffering

As a gender studies scholar, I have been frustrated over the years that the important link between the patriarchy and serious mental health problems has been slow to gain traction and prominence. *Hidden in Plain Sight* tells the truth about how sexism, gender roles, and oppression operate in our society, and how the same system that rewards men can make them dysfunctional and violent in their interpersonal relations. Feminists have been making this claim about the destructive consequences of the patriarchy for decades, but mainstream society has been slow to catch on.

I remember sitting in my kitchen in Lawrence, Kansas in 1977, ruminating about which universal concepts could explain men's gender role conflict[1,2,3,4,5]. My male clients' disclosures during therapy, plus a few psychoanalytic publications, all pointed to the fear of femininity as being a unifying concept explaining men's gender role conflict as a significant psychological problem area. I concluded that the fear of femininity was a universal part of men's psychological dynamics, and therefore it became the theoretical foundation for the concept of gender role conflict that has been empirically linked to more than forty psychological symptoms and problems[6,7]. Weiss expands my earlier work by operationalizing the fear of femininity concept. His ideas are much more practical and specific in detailing how the fears develop and impact the lives of men and women.

Advancing the Work of Psychology's Pioneers and Threats to the Status Quo

Fears of femininity and women were discussed by renowned psychoanalytic thinkers[8,9,10,11,12,13]. Some of these early luminaries actually had open conflict with each other regarding the role of masculinity and femininity in intrapsychic and interpersonal dynamics. Sigmund Freud, for example, had open and public conflicts with Alfred Adler and Carl Jung over the role of masculinity and femininity (gender roles) in causing conflict. In fact, Freud alienated Adler and Jung so much that they both left the Psychoanalytic Society in Vienna to pursue their own ideas and theories.

Unfortunately, most of these early ideas about men's fear of women and femininity were lost or abandoned over the subsequent decades since they were too threatening to the Freudian status quo and the patriarchy itself. Weiss brings us back to these lost ideas. He does so with courage as these ideas are likely to be, once again, threatening to the status quo. Writing about the fear of women is much more than "poking at the patriarchy." It is a significant threat to dismantling destructive patriarchal structures that enslave us all.

How This Book Might Impact You

This book has a positive human energy of its own, emanating from Weiss's passion and commitment to the topic. Where there is passion, there is usually excitement, depth, and new insights, and Weiss provides us with all three. He speaks authentically about gender roles and tells you how he discerned them in his own life. How invigorating for a man to express his truths with such positive vulnerability and strength.

Weiss defines and owns his truths and asks you to consider this topic's meaning in your life. The book has a planned sequence of topics to help you consider assessing the fear of women in your own life or that of someone you know. He first defines the fear of women and explains why it is important and what is at stake. Second, seven expressions of men's fears of women are discussed in the context of sexism and patriarchal structures in our society. Next, the impact of men's fears of women on society, men, women, and couples is explained. Finally, how to resolve and work through fears about women using self-help techniques, men's groups, therapy, and other resources provides a useful closing to the book.

Hidden in Plain Sight is hopeful in that Weiss believes that something can be done about men's fear of women—men can be liberated and empowered to help themselves and others. More than a self-help book, *Hidden in Plain Sight* is a valuable resource for therapists in helping men resolve their conscious and repressed fears of women and their femininity and in helping couples feel closer by resolving some of those fears. Dr. Weiss uses his therapeutic insights to create new knowledge gained by listening to clients' talk about their life experience. This kind of clinical data is sometimes devalued in academia, but therapists' insights contribute significantly to new knowledge and significant advances in mental health service delivery. Weiss' insights and ideas, just like those of Freud and Jung, represent hundreds of hours of listening to clients, completing clinical analysis, making assessments, and implementing healing interventions.

Moving Past Your Resistance

If you are a man reading this book it may stimulate your own fears of women. Your thoughts and feelings may go in two opposite directions. You might accept that indeed you have fears of women and take positive, non-defensive action. You commit to changing your attitudes and behaviors through ongoing consciousness raising or what I call "taking the gender role journey"[14,15,16]. Or, you might become defensive reading how the fear of women affects you, which may keep you from working through your psychological problems. You may resist and want to stop reading this book but not know why.

This resistance can be worked through. Hearing the truth about the patriarchy does takes courage and can uncover vulnerabilities. If the reading process is hard, get some help from others on how to turn your defensiveness into activism and personal change. The last section of the book has helpful information for men who want to work together in small groups on these issues. The bottom line is that you cannot work through your fear of women if you are resisting and defensive. Insights cannot get in if your defenses are blocking potential insights and understanding.

A Call to Action

Weiss mentions Joseph Campbell's historical period, the "great reversal." During this period of time, there was a significant shift from admiration of women to fear and disdain for women and their bodies. Women were then seen as dangerous and needing to be dominated, subordinated, and controlled in order for masculine power to be established and the patriarchy to be institutionalized. We are still living in this sexist and misogynist ideology at great costs to both men, women, and all sexual minorities.

We need another great reversal or call to action in which everyone is treated equally and there is power sharing and mutual cooperation to enhance human life, rather than letting the fear of women remain hidden in plain sight. This profound book moves us along significantly towards a better understanding of how masculinity and femininity can be experienced as human qualities rather than sexist stereotypes that victimize others and ourselves.

~~ James M. O'Neil, Ph.D.

Professor of Educational Psychology
Counselor Education, and Counseling
Psychology - University of Connecticut

Licensed Psychologist in private practice
Founding Member, Society for the Psychological Study of Men and Masculinity (SPSMM),
Division 51 of the American Psychological Association
Author-Men's Gender Role Conflict:
Psychological Costs, Consequences, and Agenda for Change (2015), American Psychological Association Books.
Gender Role Conflict Research Program
Web Page: http://web.uconn.edu/joneil/

“All men with great theories about women are afraid of women.”

~~ Barnard Werber

PREFACE

When I grudgingly recognized that I was paralyzed by my fear of the significant women in my life, I was shocked. I am sure that this statement is puzzling to the women reading this, each of whom has undoubtedly experienced themselves in a one-down, disempowered position in most of their relationships with men. Yet the truth remains that I was deeply frightened of these women in ways that have profoundly shaped the core of whom I am.

As is the case for most men, my first significant relationship with a woman was with my mother, and it took me most of my life to understand how afraid I was of her. It never occurred to me that I might be afraid of her because I was raised to hold her in such contempt. I am quite certain that my mother experienced herself as the least loved, least empowered person in the family, and she had good reason to believe that. As far as I can ascertain, my mother was profoundly unhappy for most of her life, and I experienced her unhappiness as the force that controlled the emotional life of our family. My mother abused alcohol and prescription medications when she was unhappy and would take to her bed. Incredibly, my parents arranged our home so that you had to walk through their bedroom to get to the family room in which we watched TV together. This meant that we had to walk through her unhappiness to spend any time as a family.

My mother threatened to kill herself on a regular basis, whenever the loneliness or lack of love in her life threatened to overwhelm her, I imagine. Consciously, my biggest fear was that she would kill herself and leave me feeling responsible for the rest of my life. One day, as she unleashed another in a long litany of these threats, I was filled with rage at being held hostage in this way. I told her that I knew she was full of shit and would never really kill herself. I then fled to my room and lay in my bed, terrified that I had given her the ultimate weapon with which to destroy herself, and me in the process.

More deeply buried, and far more difficult to allow myself to know and come to terms with, was the realization that my mother wished me dead. I came to know this one day, completely out of the blue, an unbidden and unwelcome thought that came to me with the shocking clarity of something you let yourself know for the first time while simultaneously recognizing it is a truth that has always been there to be known. The idea that a mother could wish her child dead might seem outlandish, but hate and love live side by side. Where you find one you will likely find the other.

What could lead a mother to wish her son dead? My mother was a bright, ambitious, highly competent woman who married and moved from her vibrant activist life in Manhattan to the suburbs of New Jersey, away from her supportive community in the city, which I believe was the death of her. As her first born, my mother turned to me to fill some of her needs for closeness and loyalty that were so painfully lacking in her marriage. Sadly, my mother was not well-equipped to bond with a child. I deeply disappointed her by emotionally allying with my father, who although intermittently and unpredictably rageful and violent, was also warm and loving towards me. This alliance left my mother feeling even more horribly despairing and alone, and I can understand why she might blame me for her suffering. I learned to defend against my mother's hatred with anger, disdain, and a faux emotional self-reliance, defenses I still instinctively turn to whenever I feel threatened by a woman.

My fears of being responsible for my mother's misery and being hated by her severely constricted my ability to experience a loving relationship with her. My next effort to find a loving relationship less constricted by fear came in the form familiar to most young adults. I sought out a romantic partner with whom I believed I could have a corrective emotional experience. I found what I was looking for, in spades. My former wife and I had a powerfully regressive bond, glomming onto each other with a fierce attachment that neither of us could really understand but both relished. We needed each other openly and voraciously, in ways that had not been possible for either of us to do in the families in which we were raised. Here, at last, was a love I could indulge in fully and without fear.

What neither of us had the maturity to understand at the time is how much easier it is to surrender unconsciously to that kind of deliciously regressive dependency than it is to work your way consciously out of it to a more mature relationship. Years passed before we had our first significant conflict, but when we did, we were both horribly wounded to discover that we were completely unable to work our way through it. In some ways we really never recovered from that painful recognition of our separateness and were never able to build a mature connection that included an integration of our differences.

I remarried several years ago and am happy to report that I am more secure and less ruled by fear in this relationship than in any of my previous intimate relationships with women. I've had a lot of good therapy, and the work I've done on this book has been very helpful to me. Nonetheless, it is also important to understand the lingering power of these issues for many men.

It is still true for me that whenever my wife and I are in conflict, if I get emotionally activated enough, I still instinctively go right back to the same defenses of anger, disdain, and self-reliance that I learned to use with my mother, the same defenses that protect me against realizing how scared I am.

~~ Avrum G. Weiss, Ph.D.

HIDDEN

in

PLAIN SIGHT

There is one fear, above all others, that unites men. . . It's a fear that affects almost all men, whether they are meek and timid by nature or the kind men who walk into burning buildings to save people's lives. It includes professional boxers, commercial fishermen, inner city police officers, government whistleblowers and law enforcement agents who infiltrate organized crime.

It is not a fear of death that cripples them, nor of torture or personal ruin. But it is a fear so great their refusal to face it has driven them at worst to kill themselves and others. . . That fear is the fear of losing a woman's love and approval.

~~ Paul Elam

Introduction

I've worked with a lot of men in psychotherapy, which is unusual because men are often generally reluctant to seek therapy. I've spent a lot time sitting and listening to men, engaged in deeply intimate conversation with them. As I listened, it became increasingly clearer to me that most of the men I worked with were afraid of their partners. Much of what they talked about in therapy was how unhappy they felt in their relationships and how absolutely helpless and hopeless they felt to do anything about it.

I started suggesting to men that it sounded like they were afraid of their partners. I intentionally used the words "scared" and "afraid" to evoke the feeling and make it more present in the room as we talked. Each time, the man I was talking to would first look either perplexed or irritated at my suggesting that he was afraid of a woman. That lasted an average of thirty seconds before a slowly dawning look of recognition came over his face and he said words to the effect of "I never thought about it that way, but you're right. I am afraid of her."

This new understanding of the interior lives of men and their intimate relationships has been tremendously helpful to me, to my male patients, and to their intimate partners. Seeing their experience through this lens has helped a lot of men be more intimate with their female partners and in their friendships with other men.

Developing a more in-depth understanding of men's fears of women in intimate relationships has also been of great interest to many women. Heterosexual women, in particular, are often very interested in understanding the internal lives of men, and there are a number of best-selling books purporting to do just that. Because their male partners are generally reluctant to talk about their internal lives, particularly with their female partners, these women often experience their partners as opaque, an enigma. Their partners' intransigent reluctance, or inability, to talk about themselves is one of the greatest sources of dissatisfaction for many women in intimate relationships with men. I hope that men will give this book to their female intimate partners and their daughters as the start of a conversation that deepens their understanding of each other, and that women will give the book to their male intimate partners and sons with the same intent.

In addition to helping effect individual change, and effecting change in relationships, I also think of this book as a contribution to the larger feminist movement for gender equality and social justice. The interplay between individual and larger sociocultural factors in any phenomenon is complex and often controversial. Men's fears of intimate relationships are clearly one manifestation of the larger patriarchy, a pervasive system created by men to maintain their privilege. From this perspective, men's fears of women can be understood as the inevitable insecurity that all people who gain their advantage through power or coercion necessarily have to live with.

The graphic above represents this dilemma for men. The man is on top, but the woman has one foot off of the seesaw, and he has to live with the fear that she can bring him down at any time.

As a psychotherapist, I am also interested in the unconscious factors underlying social problems such as the patriarchy. Helping men and their intimate partners become more aware of men's fears of women in intimate relationships is not by itself sufficient to create social change, but it is an important step in the process of change.

The primary focus of this book is to develop a better understanding of men's fears of women in intimate relationships. Men are less frightened of women in the external world because they have managed to create a world in which they largely dominate and control women by convincing themselves that they don't need women. This allows men to exert power and control over women in the external world largely without ambivalence, what researchers have called "hostile sexism."[17]

While men may have convinced themselves that they do not need women in the external world, at home is a different story. It is in intimate relationships that men's fears of women are most activated and most visible. Most men are consciously aware of needing their partners for things like the need to have a reliable sexual partner and someone to take the bulk of the responsibility for raising the children, running the home and family, and managing the family's social life.[18] Men also have more subtle needs in their intimate relationships with women that they are often largely or completely unaware of. Such needs include the need for someone to share with emotionally, and someone to be supported and comforted by in ways that men do not generally have available from other men.

In intimate relationships, each person is at least partially dependent on the other person's cooperation and ongoing investment to get their needs met.[19] There is at least some level of interdependency and awareness of the interpersonal consequences of pursuing one's own needs without regard to the impact on another. The mutual interdependency of intimate relationships constrains the power of each person, but particularly the person who has been in the more dominant position. This is particularly problematic for men who believe that losing power in an intimate relationship with a woman is shaming[20] and that their female partner will use their dependency to control, manipulate, and exploit them.[21] These men feel more threatened and provoked and respond more defensively when they believe their partners are challenging their decisions.[22]

In an attempt to resolve the dilemma of needing the interdependency of an intimate relationship and fearing the accompanying loss of power and control, many heterosexual men adopt an ambivalent, benevolent sexism towards their intimate partners.[23] In this benevolent sexism, men tend to venerate and idealize women in their roles as wives and mothers and idealize them as romantic love objects, while continuing to exclude women from the kind of agentic roles that might threaten men's dominance in the larger world. Benevolent sexism perpetuates the belief that women are not as capable in agentic settings and allows men to justify their domination in a paternalistic way, i.e., believing they have to take care of women because they are not fully capable of taking care of themselves. This dyadic dependency that men have on women creates an unusual situation in which members of a more powerful group are dependent on a subordinate group for some of their most personal needs,[24] similar to the ways that white women in the South have depended on Black women to raise their children.

"Segregation scars the soul of the perpetrator as well as the perpetrated."

~~ Dr. Martin Luther King

It is controversial, some would say offensive or even dangerous, to suggest that those in privileged positions are also harmed by the systems they create to oppress others. There is a long-standing controversy within feminism about the importance versus the dangers of talking about the ways in which men are also impacted by patriarchy.[25] I have been approached, rather forcefully at times, and with a lot of emotion, by dear and trusted friends and colleagues who have suggested that it is irresponsible of me to write this book because it will be used to justify bad behavior by men. This is a legitimate concern. It is treacherous to write about the ways in which an abusive system also impacts perpetrators—in this case, the ways in which men are also harmed by the patriarchy—without sounding like you are crying "white tears," a colloquial term meant to poke fun at white people who feel guilty or defensive when confronted with their privilege. For example, white people complain about being discriminated against by affirmative action or declare that "all lives matter," or Christians in the United States complain about being the victims of religious persecution. The fear my friends and colleagues have expressed is that understanding will lead to forgiveness, that painting men's bad behavior in a sympathetic light will be taken for condoning the behavior, for shedding "white tears."

It is also true, historically, that when men have entered the conversation to talk about their experience, they quickly become the center of that conversation and the voices of women are often lost. The Supreme Court confirmation hearings of Brett Kavanaugh are an excellent example. As long as Dr. Ford was alone in talking about her experience, most of those listening—including the President and a majority of Republican senators—said they found her testimony credible. However, as soon as Justice Kavanaugh and Senator Lindsay Graham made the strategic decision to go on the offensive and put their own experience front and center in an angry and entitled way, they appropriated the role of sympathetic victim and Dr. Ford's voice was quickly lost.

There are also those who take men's legitimate fears of women and conflate them into an understanding of the world in which women have all the power and men are disadvantaged and persecuted.[26] There is no reasonable understanding of the world that rationally supports that conclusion. Men still retain the majority of power in the world and in almost any heterosexual relationship. It is the birthright that both men and women inherit, willingly or unwillingly, from their families and the patriarchal culture they grew up in, and straight couples have to work unceasingly to stem the patriarchal tide that resides deeply within both of them in order to find any hope of a mutual partnership.

It is confusing when people in privileged positions talk about being afraid. We think of fear as something that only people in disadvantaged positions experience and imagine that the advantages of privilege inoculate against fear. It is all too easy to think about privilege in a relationship in two-dimensional terms, reducing the complexity of the relational patterns to two roles, a victim and a perpetrator. It is challenging to validate the emotional experience of those in the privileged position without appearing to condone the controlling behaviors that often mask their fears. When someone talks about being afraid, we instinctively think there must be someone to blame, someone who is responsible for frightening them. The challenge is to talk about men's fears of women without blaming women. Men are afraid of women not because of something that women have done to them, but because of the patriarchy in which both men and women live.

The feminist principle of mutuality states that a relationship can only be growth-enhancing for one person if it is growth-enhancing for both, and by extension, that a relationship is detrimental to both parties if it is detrimental or limiting to either one.[27] While men clearly are the primary beneficiaries of the patriarchy, they are also harmed by the same system that harms women, harmed by the limitations the patriarchy imposes on men's capacity to lead fully emotional lives and participate in mutual relationships. The American Psychological Association's "Guidelines for Psychological Practice with Boys and Men"[28] acknowledges the privilege given to men and boys and their greater degree of social and economic power, while also saying that men are confined and restricted in their capacity to adaptively function by the same system-level policies that bestow that power. Men's "lives are a strange combination of power and pain, privilege and isolation. The way we define our power, the way we have set up a world of men's power, the way we assert that power – these are the sources of our pain; this is men's contradictory experience of power".[29]

Back to the graphic earlier in this introduction. Men do understand that as soon as the woman figures out how to extricate herself from her one-down position, he'll come tumbling down. He's OK only as long as she's OK. For women, or any other group of disempowered people, stepping off the bottom of the seesaw is never as easy as some might think. Women in abusive relationships leave an average of seven times before leaving for good.[30,31]

When we stereotypically reduce our understanding of men in intimate relationships as commitment-phobic, emotionally withholding, or shut down, we do a disservice to men and profoundly misunderstand what is happening in the couple. When we understand the fears that lie beneath these defensive postures in men, then everything changes. The only way out of this mess is to work together. We are going to have to include an interest in the internal lives of men if we—women and men together—are ever to work our way out of the grip of the patriarchy.

A Note About Same-Sex Couples

As a heterosexual man married to a woman, I have tried to be sensitive to my unconscious tendency to view couples' issues through my own, heteronormative lens. I use heteronormative language, i.e., terms like "couple" to refer only to heterosexual couples, or to a man's "partner" only as a woman. I am aware that in doing so I risk recreating trauma for LBGTQ+ people by making heteronormative assumptions about what couples look like. That is not my intent. Gay men's fears of women and fears in non-binary or gender-fluid intimate relationships are different dynamics than those of cisgender men, and I am not qualified to write about those dynamics.

Many of the dynamics described in this book do not occur in the same ways in same sex couples who do not have the particular emotional intensity that arises for men who are partnered to someone who is the same gender as their mother. However, same sex couples do have the same internal conflicts and fears about dependency in intimate relationships.

Use of Language

Precise language is particularly critical for this project. Talking about men's fears of women is rife with potential misunderstandings and even landmines. I am not so naïve to believe that I can avoid all offense or misunderstandings simply by addressing the issue of language at the beginning of this book, but perhaps we can at least get off on the right foot together.

- The clinical term for men's fears of women is gynophobia, which is a social phobia. In the past, the Latin term "horror feminae" was used.[32] This is different from misogyny, which is a hatred of, or prejudice against, women rather than a fear, although the two are very much related as we will discuss later in the book. A related concept is femiphobia, a term coined by psychologist Steven Ducat, meaning fear of feminine traits in men.[33]

- My use of the words "scared" or "afraid" may be off-putting to some men. When I use these words with men they often dilute what I've said by substituting a less threatening word to describe their feelings, such as "concerned" or "worried." "Scared" and "afraid," however, not only most accurately describe the feelings men have, they most powerfully evoke those feelings in men and help them bring those feelings into the room. Most men are initially defensive about the suggestion that they are afraid of anything, much less afraid of a woman, because they have been socialized to believe that it is not masculine to be afraid of a woman. But they quickly settle into acknowledging that what they are experiencing is fear, and it helps them to move deeper into their experience, and it is often fairly quickly comforting to acknowledge being scared and relieving to let go of the burden of pretending they are not.
- I use the term "partner" to refer to all intimate romantic relationships because it is the most inclusive term.
- One unavoidable limitation of writing about such a broad topic is that I have painted with a broad-brush stroke and made broad stereotypical judgments that are not always flattering to men or equally applicable across some younger generations and subcultures. Not all men, and someday we hope not even most men, will recognize themselves in all these broad descriptions of

what men are like. It is my experience from tens of thousands of hours of in-depth therapeutic work with men, that the vast majority of heterosexual men recognize very quickly what I am talking about, and that they experience that recognition as freeing rather than binding.

Connecting With Other Readers

There is information at the end of Chapter Fifteen about how to connect with other readers who are interested in this topic.

Men are afraid that women will laugh at them.
Women are afraid that men will kill them.

~~ Margaret Atwood

Section I

What Do Men's Fears of Women Look Like?

The classic "Still Face" developmental psychology experiment[34] begins with a mother and her infant child playing with each other as they normally do. The split screen makes it clear that they are in a conversation, each learning which funny faces and silly noises best elicit a smile from the other. At a certain point, the mothers are instructed to turn away from their babies, and when they turn back, to have a "still face," meaning to not show any emotion or respond to their babies in any way. Almost immediately the babies become wary and escalate their efforts to reengage their mothers. Within minutes of these attempts failing, the babies start crying hysterically, so distressed that some of them lose bodily control. Male infants are more distressed than female infants in the study. They show more facial expressions of anger and are more likely to try to escape the situation.[35] The experimenters concluded that the male infants need more help from their female caregivers to regulate their emotions. The male infants' terrified wails of impotent protest are repeated in various forms in men's fears in intimate relationships with women.

Men afraid of women? How can that be true? It's pretty clear that women are justified in their fears of men. Men hold positions of privilege and power in most personal and professional settings, and thirty-five percent of women worldwide experience physical and/or sexualized violence from a man in their lifetime.[36] It is counter-intuitive, and some would say offensive and even dangerous, to talk about men being afraid of women. Men are so strongly socialized to hide any signs of fear that their fears of women are largely hidden from women, from other men, and from themselves. The great paradox of men's lives is that they "have all the power but do not feel powerful."[37] The chapters in this section explore specific ways those fears play out, first in everyday life, and then in the world at large.

Notes

"We have to talk about the trouble with men. We have to understand why they fear women so much."

~~ Meryl Streep

CHAPTER ONE

HIDDEN IN PLAIN SIGHT: MEN'S FEARS OF WOMEN IN EVERYDAY LIFE

Men's fears of women in intimate relationships are hidden in plain sight. Most men do such an incredibly good job at hiding these fears and vulnerabilities that even their mothers and lovers don't know how scared they are. Men hide their fears because they are taught that real men don't get scared, and that if they do, they should never let anyone know because they will lose respect and be at a competitive disadvantage with other men. You should not let women know because they will think less of you as a man and be less attracted to you, or may even take advantage of you. Hiding these fears is so reflexive for most men that they are largely unaware of them. They are, however, just below the surface, and it doesn't take much prompting to recognize them. One man said to me, "At first I passed by it, because I thought 'I'm not afraid of women.' But since that moment my mind's been racing, thinking of the ways that can be true and has been true as far back as I remember."

It is much easier for men to hide their fears of women out in the world at large than in the less guarded moments of their private lives when they are more openly themselves. Intimate partners make more intentional efforts to be more open and vulnerable with each other than they are in public. As a result, men's fears of women show up much differently at home than they do out in the world.

Men's fears of women are most likely to be stimulated in any situation in which men encounter a woman who has more authority than they do, shows evidence of being strong or competent, evidence of being self-confident, or shows that she is angry.[38] For example, research suggests that the more competent a woman is at work the less likable she is rated by the men that work there.[39]

Fifty years ago, psychiatrist Wolfgang Lederer[40] wrote these examples of men's fears of women, and while the socio-cultural context has changed, the core of these fears is remarkably consistent. "A lawyer races his sports-car home, lest his wife accuse him of dawdling . . . A full-sized man has nightmares that his wife, in bed, will roll on him and crush him . . . A car salesman, single, is afraid to be roped in, and a wine merchant, married, is afraid of being kicked out by their respective women".[41] Lederer added a quote from one of his patients. "A woman's anger is to be feared because she can throw a man out of the house. She can also kill him. She can not only cut off his balls but can kill him: that's what my mother did to my father—from the day she kicked him out of the house to the day he lay on the slab he steadily went downhill."

Here are some more contemporary examples of the ways that men's fears of women show up in intimate relationships. If you are a man reading this, see how far down the list you get before you start to recognize yourself and/or your relationship. Show these examples to a few of your male friends and colleagues and watch their expression shift from puzzled to a dawning recognition.

- You are a man in a committed relationship with a woman. Friends ask you at the last minute to get together and have a drink after work. You and your partner don't have any plans for the evening, and it bothers you that your first thought is not about whether you would like to see your friends but about whether your partner will be upset with you. She has never objected to your getting together with your friends—this is not a group of guys who get together to go to strip clubs or chase women—and yet even after calling to check in with her, it's hard to shake the feeling that you've done something wrong. You want to feel free, unencumbered.
- You are a man in a committed relationship with a woman. You and your partner come home at the end of the day and it seems clear to you that she is upset. You ask if she's OK, and she insists that she is. You ask if she's upset with you, and she assures you she is not. Despite all of her reassurance, you can't quite shake an uneasy, unsettled feeling. The longer she stays upset, the more worried you get, until her being upset becomes your single preoccupation, as if nothing else can happen until that is resolved. You are convinced that she is upset with you, that you've done something

"wrong," although you have no idea what that might be. You yearn to feel off the hook and back to the status quo.

- You are a man and a woman in a committed relationship, having an argument. As the woman, you are hurt and angry. As the man, you can clearly see that she's upset, and her tears make you surprisingly uncomfortable. While you would like to feel empathic, there is something about her strong feelings that is distressing to you and gets in the way. Because you are uncomfortable with your own strong feelings, you, the man, begin to withdraw emotionally and detach to protect yourself. For reasons you don't fully understand, it becomes increasingly important to you to remain rational and unemotional, and you are increasingly critical of, and irritated with, your partner for being "too emotional." You, the woman, can feel your partner withdrawing, and the more he withdraws, the stronger your feelings become and the more urgently you pursue him, trying to find a way to make some kind of emotional connection. Now you both are locked in a mutually destructive cycle; the more you, the woman, push for the emotional connection you yearn for, the more he detaches. The more you, the man, try to control your fear by detaching, the more upset she gets.
- You are a man and woman in a long-term committed relationship. Your sexual relationship started out pretty hot and exciting. You had a lot of sex, both enjoyed it, and seemed to agree about wanting to have sex as often as you could. Over the last few years, not only has the

frequency fallen way off, but sex has started to feel more like just another thing to check off the list. Neither of you is very excited about it; it's just something you both feel like you should do. Although you, as the man, find yourself less interested in sex with your partner, you still feel very sexually alive. You are often turned on by other women and masturbate frequently, usually to images of women who don't look much like your partner and to sexual activities that are different from the sex you have with her. You are particularly turned on by scenes in which the woman's desire is very overt, but when your partner is open about her own sexual desire, you get turned off. Truth be told, it often seems more attractive to masturbate to fantasies you can control than to navigate the complex emotional territory that's become necessary to have sex with your partner. For you as the woman, although your partner is an attentive lover, generous in his attention to your pleasure, there is no passion in the love-making. What you crave is to feel desired.

One man gave this example of his powerful life-shaping fears of women:

My wife snored at night, and no matter what I tried I could not sleep when she was snoring. She did finally get a sleep study done, which confirmed a severe, life-threatening case of sleep apnea. It was another year before she got a CPAP machine, and for that year, I lay next to her every night, rageful at her for keeping me awake. Now here's the kicker. My son had already left for college, and there was an empty bedroom right down the hall. I was so afraid of my wife's disapproval that I chose to lay there every night, steeped in my own rage, rather than getting up and taking care of myself by simply moving to another room.

Let's turn our attention now to how men's fears of women are visible in the culture.

Notes

"If you want something said, ask a man. If you want something done, ask a woman."

~~ Margaret Thatcher

"A man does what he can; a woman does what a man cannot."

~~ Isabel Allende, *Inés of My Soul*

Chapter Two

Men's Fears of Women in the Larger Context

People generally strive to control what they feel threatened by. The simplest and most compelling evidence of men's fears of women is the patriarchy that dominates so much of our lives. If men didn't fear women there would be no need to devise a system to dominate and control them. The same could be said about men using violence to control women. An abusive man will often protest that his partner "made me do it," unintentionally (and incorrectly) betraying his belief that he can be controlled by women.

Men's Fears of Women in History and Myth

First oral myths, and then written history, have been primarily told and written by men. As long as men have been the ones telling the story, they have been talking about their fears of women. In every culture, men have "disparaged and feared women almost as vigorously as they have adored and pursued them."[42] Women have often been portrayed as "contaminating, iniquitous personifications of danger and evil."[43] Even in contemporary Western cultures women are portrayed as "temptresses, maliciously bent on perverting reason, swaying men from righteousness, defiling all that is sacred and pure, and undermining the moral fabric of culture."[44]

In pre-agrarian, hunter-gatherer times, the individual household was the primary unit, and women by virtue of their reproductive and childrearing roles dominated the household. People naturally worshipped goddesses. With the domestication of animals and farming, populations became more stationary. Men no longer needed to be absent to hunt for such long periods of time. People built cities with higher levels of organization than the individual family, and the best interests of the tribe or community superseded the best interests of any individual family. Organized societies from the beginning were societies of men, with male gods.

Joseph Campbell calls this period "the great reversal,"[45] during which there was a shift from admiration of women to a fear and disdain for women, their bodies, and nature as the symbolic mother. Women begin to be depicted as dangerous to men, often by seducing them. The first book of the bible tells the story of a woman, Eve, betraying her partner and causing them to be exiled from the utopian garden and forced to fend for themselves. The Greek version is Pandora, who was created by Zeus to punish humans for stealing fire, and who then unleashes for all eternity evil, sickness, and death on humankind. The Greek story of Odysseus, written three thousand years ago, is the story of a man who spent ten years overcoming a series of unimaginably difficult obstacles in female form, only to return home, from the Sirens who used their sexuality to try and lure Odysseus to his ruin on the rocks, to Circe the enchantress who similarly used her beauty and threatened to "unman" him.[46] Delilah seduced Sampson and brought him to ruin. The most dangerous characters in fairy tales are most often either a woman as a seductress or as a mother or stepmother. Lederer reviewed two-hundred of Grimm's fairy tales and found 52 dangerous female characters and only six dangerous male characters.[47]

Throughout history, men have feared what is mysterious about women.[48] Most cultures have taboos against menstruation, pregnancy, and childbirth. Women experiencing these things are generally considered dangerous, contagious, and able to cause weakness in men and so are segregated. In preindustrial cultures men commonly sealed themselves off from women before hunts or wars, believing that contact with women might make them weaker.[49] Interestingly, one can find remnants of this same idea in the superstition held by some athletes that having sex before the big game will make them weaker.

Many cultures around the world have some story, image, or symbol of a vagina with teeth, *vagina dentata*, so that intercourse risks emasculation.[50] Psychoanalyst Karen Horney suggested that every male patient had dreams about the fear of the vagina.[51] There are some animal species that engage in sexual cannibalism in which the female kills the male after mating, including the female praying mantis who bites off the head of her male lover.

One of the most dramatic eruptions of men's fears of women was the persecution of women as witches by the Catholic Church, which continued for more than five-hundred years, beginning in the mid-13th century.[52] Estimates vary, but some believe that up to one-hundred thousand women were murdered during this time.[53] One Spanish inquisitor boasted that in the century and a half from 1400, at least 30,000 witches were burned.[54] In the bishopric of Trier in 1585, the inquisitors left only one female inhabitant alive in each of two villages.

Another important development in the ongoing evolution of men's fears of women was the large19th century shift in how manhood was defined and achieved in America.[55] Men felt threatened by the potential loss of their privileged positions in various areas, leading to the escalation of femiphobia nationally. Early industrialization took fathers away from work in the home to work in factories and offices. Male self-employment fell from 67 percent in 1870 to 37 percent in 1910.[56] Fathers became less present in their son's lives.

At the same time, women began to enter the workforce in increasing numbers and there was a general sense that gender roles were changing in a way that devalued roles that had traditionally belonged to men, leading to an increase in men's anxiety about the security of their positions as men.

A variety of organizations emerged at this time to counter the feared feminizing effect on boys and men, including the YMCA and the Boy Scouts of America.[57] In 1897, one in five men belonged to a fraternal lodge.[58] Competitive sports became another popular all-male refuge for developing masculinity, particularly the ritualized combat of football.

An interesting and more recent manifestation of men's fears of women can be found in the genre of horror films. The primary audience for horror movies is adolescent boys. They are successful, like ghost stories and fairy tales, to the extent they engage our repressed fears and desires and reenact our unconscious conflicts about those fears.[59] In many of the classics, *Alien, The Brood, The Exorcist,* and *Sisters*, evil is represented by feminine forms that threaten to kill or mutilate men. In all these cases, women's sexuality seems to be at the root of men's fears just as it was in earlier myths and fairytales.[60] In *Carrie*, the hit Stephen King movie of 1976, Carrie is horribly teased by a prank played by the girls at the senior prom in which they pretend she is the prom queen and then dump a bucket of blood on her. This was prompted by Carrie having her period in the locker room and not knowing what it was. However, her beginning menses gives her powerful telekinetic powers, which she uses to enact revenge against the whole class. King says the movie was a success because it appeals to anyone who has been an adolescent boy and had the experience or fear of having his gym shorts pulled down, which the author equates to a fear of castration or genital mutilation by other men.

Another manifestation of men's fears of women in the psychiatric community is the creation of the Borderline Personality Disorder diagnosis, which I like to say is from the Latin meaning "I'm scared to death of you and it's all your fault." One of the few times that men are comfortable acknowledging their fears of women is when the women are labeled as Borderline, a category so fearful, so powerful that no man can stand against them. They are vicious, untreatable, and the only effective strategy is the magical amulet of "boundaries," meaning devices to keep as far away as possible, or better yet, to hurt them before they have a chance to hurt you. It is the profession's way of rationalizing men's fears of women's strong emotions.

Anecdotally, I and other therapists are seeing a significant increase in Inhibited Sexual Desire (ISD) in men, which can be another reflection of their fears of women. As we will take up in more detail in Chapter Seven, most of what young men learn today about sex and sexuality comes from pornography. The women they are dating make it clear that for them, sexuality follows from an emotional connection, but the porn they are watching depicts women surrendering to uncontrollable desire in response to men who are dominant to the point of being aggressive. Add the long overdue #MeToo movement to speak out about male sexual exploitation and abuse, and men are overwhelmingly confused about what it means to be a man sexually, and how to please their partners.

The final, and by far most disturbing current manifestation of men's fears of women is the advent of the New Men's Movement. While the original men's movement of the 1960s framed itself as feminist and allies of women, this men's movement is shockingly hostile toward women or anything related to the feminine. Any man in this movement who identifies as a feminist is attacked as a traitor, a "feminazi." There is a large online group called Men Going Their Own Way (MGTOW), which advocates men learning to live their lives without needing women in any way. Their paranoid vision is of a world that is "gynocentric," with men as victims of a system that favors women and persecutes men. Some of their more fanciful claims include that there is no such thing as a wage gap, that marriage is a form of slavery for men, that men are arrested in domestic violence disputes even when the woman has clearly been the aggressor, and that men have been forced to pay child support for children proven by DNA evidence not to be their biological children.

One man in a Facebook group wrote, "A woman through one false statement can invariably ruin a man's life, and the common response is to make statements like 'pick yourself up and keep going' or 'you can't control others only how you react'." Another man shared:

> *Men do not have a disproportionate share of power in the world, that's feminist theory, and not supported by observable reality . . . Women on aggregate do tend to be judgmental and overly critical of men. . . Typically it's the female partner who loses interest in sex, or starts rationing it to control your behavior, it's one of many forms of manipulation. Basically, the default model of relationship(s) in the West is that of man as a supplicant trying to appease a petty tyrant of a partner who will have it HER WAY, or no way, with little if any effort on her part to reciprocate, once she has you locked in.*

Attorneys specializing in helping men with divorce profit from stoking men's fears about how they will be taken advantage of in the process and need their help. I think that, or I should say, I hope that, the majority of you reading this are shocked and horrified by these claims. I can tell you that I spent a weekend lost in this dark online world, and I ended up literally fleeing, literally fearing for my own safety.

Section II

The Progression of Men's Fears of Women

The chapters in this section illustrate a progression in men's fears of women, starting with those fears that are the most conscious and moving progressively towards those that are largely unconscious, while also moving from the fears that are more socially acceptable and more likely to be acknowledged by men and recognized by women towards those that are less socially desirable and more likely to be hidden by men from others and from themselves.

Every classification system by necessity over generalizes. Most heterosexual men experience some version of these seven fears but not every man's experience fits neatly into one of these seven categories. The seven categories are theoretical constructs, designed to try to summarize lived experience to make it easier to talk about and understand.

“When men imagine a female uprising, they imagine a world in which women rule men as men have ruled women.”

~~ Sally Kempton in
Meditation for the Love of It

CHAPTER THREE

MEN ARE AFRAID OF BEING DOMINATED OR CONTROLLED BY WOMEN

Pussy-whipped. Why is it that one of the worst things a man can be accused of is being controlled by a woman, or more accurately, controlled by his need for a woman? Men's fears of being dominated and controlled by women is the most socially acceptable of men's fears of women and, therefore, is the one that men and their partners are most likely to be aware of. There is no more convincing evidence of men's fears of being dominated and controlled by women than their insistent protestations that they are not. In fact, men's fears of being dominated by women is readily visible in the culture in the numerous jokes about it—jokes about not letting the woman wear the pants in the family, about men not being allowed to speak in their relationships, etc. If you ask any man if he is afraid of being controlled by his partner, he will, of course, adamantly deny it. He might tell you that he is angry about her attempts to control him, but scared is probably not a word that comes readily to his mind, and certainly not the word he would use to describe himself to anyone else. The fact that it is so important to most men to continually reassure themselves and others that they are not controlled by women clearly reflects their underlying fears that they are. As Shakespeare famously wrote "The lady doth protest too much, methinks."[61]

The old-fashioned term "henpecked" was used as far back as 1671 by the English poet and satirist Samuel Butler.

> *The henpecked man rides behind his wife let her wear the spurs and govern the reins . . . He is subordinate and ministerial to his wife, who commands his chief, and he dares to nothing without her order . . . He changes sexes with his wife, and put off the old man to put on the new woman. She sits at the helm, and he does but tug like a slave at the oar.*[62]

Notice how men being dominated by women is equated with being emasculated, "He changes sexes with his wife," and the subtle eroticism in the reference to being ridden with spurs. Also striking is how little has changed in over 250 years. If the language were updated, we could find many of these same sentiments expressed by many men today. Here is a recent excerpt from a comedian.[63]

> *I just find women to be relentless. Every day they wake up and they just come at you. They have an agenda, they are like these psycho robots that never run out of batteries, and every day they just keep coming at you. You gotta deal with that every single day. . . I mean literally, you know, every day, it's like waves hitting the beach. Every day, just eroding a little more of your life away. Just waking up, inch by inch, every day, "why are you hanging out with him, he drinks too much?"*

"Where did you find that? That's ugly, throw it out." Until one day you are just hanging out in the middle of a lagoon, just swimming there with your baseball cards, you're waving to your friends back on the shore, "don't get me tickets, I still like sports! Oh, here she comes, here she comes. "Hi honey!"

Men are socialized to see themselves, and frequently look for ways to prove to others, that they are independent to the point of being self-reliant, that they don't need help from anybody, that they are their own man and not influenced by others. They mock each other about having to ask their partners permission to do anything, projecting their own fears onto other men in order to reassure themselves. Notice how much of men's ridiculing of each involves accusations about being more feminine, in other words, less masculine. For example, when a man talks about a woman trying to control him, he may say that she "emasculates" him, or is a "ballbuster."

Woman destroys man's superiority, she sets about mutilating, dominating man, she contradicts him, she denies his truth and his values.

~~ Simone Beauvoir in *The Second Sex*

Men's Silence

In these stereotypical views of heterosexual relationships, women are portrayed as dominating and controlling, and men are presented as compliant and afraid to speak up about what they want. There is an old Jewish joke in which a young boy comes home from school, very excited to tells his mother that he got a part in the school play. "What part?" his mother asks. "I'm playing the role of the Jewish husband," replies the boy. His mother, clearly upset, replies, "You go back and tell that teacher you want a speaking part!"

Psychologist Dana Jack is well known for her work on the patriarchal pressures on women to silence themselves in intimate relationships, and the resultant emotional, physiological, and sociocultural costs.[64] Jack agrees that although the causes and costs are different, men also struggle not to silence themselves in intimate relationships. My clinical experience supports the idea that men tend to be more reticent than their female partners in opening up about their internal lives. In most therapy with heterosexual couples, it is the woman who takes the lead in being more emotionally open. If the therapy goes well, the man follows her lead and matches her vulnerability.

There are two significant issues that impede men from speaking up in their intimate relationships with women. The first is shame.[65] Men are particularly reluctant to speak up about their own needs and desires in relationships with women because they have been socialized to feel ashamed of needing anything from anyone. The second problem for men in speaking up is the fear of abandonment. Men understand that speaking up about their needs may result in things getting better in their relationship, but there is also the risk that speaking up will make things worse, maybe even much worse. This is an important dynamic in the relationships between men and women that we will take up in more detail in Chapter Sixteen.

Bill and Jane came to see me when their marriage was already in serious trouble. Bill was quiet, introverted, and reluctant to say much to me or his wife about what was going on inside of him. Jane was just the opposite: outgoing, frequently speaking her mind without giving much thought to how her words might affect whomever she was talking to. As you might imagine, Bill and Jane's relationship was quite volatile. Bill traveled frequently for work, but even when he was home, Jane frequently felt painfully alone. The harder and louder she pushed for some connection with Bill, the more withdrawn and silent he got. I decided to have an individual session with each of them. When Bill and I were alone, he started unwinding years' worth of frustrations and dissatisfactions about the marriage. Stunned, I asked Bill how much of this he had talked about with his wife. Bill looked at me blankly, as if that were the craziest idea he had ever heard. Bill had not talked about any single part of what was troubling him to Jane and had no intention of ever doing so. As far as Bill was concerned, Jane was already so angry at him without him telling her any of what was bothering him, that he couldn't imagine risking the explosion he was sure would follow if he actually told her some of what was on his mind. Within a few months, Bill and Jane had another explosive argument that was deeply disturbing to both of them. Jane decided she couldn't take any more and asked Bill for a divorce. Bill has still not told her anything about what was going wrong for him in their relationship, and at this point, it is unlikely he ever will.

The Parent-Child Relationship

> *Like a conductor zipping up a piece of music, Julia gave a quick and stern "Enough," and that was it. What was so scary about her? What about that five-foot-four woman, who never inflicted physical or*
>
> *emotional violence, or even saw a punishment all the way through, terrified her husband and children to the point of unconditional surrender? Here I Am.*
>
> ~~Jonathon Safran Foer

Over time, many heterosexual relationships begin to take on characteristics more reflective of the relationship between a parent and child than a partnership between two adults. The pattern is common enough for therapists to have named it "the parent-child relationship." In heterosexual relationships, it is most often the woman who ends up in the role of the adult, taking responsibility for everything, and the man in the role of the passive aggressive, acting-out child. This pattern is often easily visible in the first few minutes of a psychotherapy session with a couple. I always start sessions by asking "How are you? It's an open-ended question to both people, an invitation to talk in a more personal way about themselves or the relationship. When I ask that question of couples, the man invariably either looks to his partner for the answer or answers very timidly and immediately checks with her to see if he's gotten it right. Clearly, in many heterosexual couples there in an unspoken agreement that the woman is the authority about how things are going in the relationship.

Men joke with each other about how they live as bachelors, that there's nothing but beer and pizza in their refrigerator, what a mess their apartments are, and how they are beholden to no one, free to do whatever they want whenever they want. Underneath the bragging, there is a recognition that a lot of men don't know much about how to make a home for themselves or raise a family. For most men, not much was expected of them as a child in either area, so they didn't get much experience doing the work or even noticing what needs doing and taking responsibility for getting it done. While men joke about wanting to live the bachelor life and resenting having a woman trying to socialize them, on some level they appreciate the changes that a woman can bring into their lives. It feels good to live someplace that feels more like the home they grew up in, to have a more regular life they can count on and relax into, to have a reliable social life that is taken care of for them, and to have someone help soothe their anxiety about not knowing what to wear or how to act in more grownup social situations. Underneath the joking and resentment, men are often grateful for a little benign guidance. Men also understand that making a home and raising a family are often very important to their partners; being willing to follow a few instructions seems like a small price to pay for the critically important approval they seek from them.

When it goes well, as it often does in the beginning of a relationship, this is a great example of how couples can help each other learn and become more fully themselves, to live more completely into the full potential of who they are. However, what starts as a mutually beneficial implicit agreement can deteriorate into a series of unspoken power struggles. The pattern is dissatisfying to both partners, but the dissatisfaction is most likely to surface first with the woman. Many women recognize that they have a lot more experience and expertise in relationships than their male partners. Women joke about men not being a good fit off the rack and needing alteration, or about having to train their partners. On the surface, most of the guidance and coaching they offer to their partners is about how to behave, but what women are really looking for is not a partner who is better trained, but a partner who is better at connection, better at intimacy.

Here's the critical turning point. When men understand what their partner is really looking for and recognize that they might actually want the same thing, they are less likely to be defensive and less reactive to the coaching and prodding they are receiving, and things usually go well. On the other hand, when men miss the larger point, when they have such a paucity of positive early attachment experiences that they don't recognize, or are not drawn to, the closeness their partners are offering, then all of the formerly benign guidance and coaching begins to chafe and seem more and more like criticism and control.

When that happens, men start to feel like the relationship has become a rigged game; no matter how much they try to help, no matter how much they defer to the way she wants things done and work like hell to have everything the way she wants it, it seems like nothing they ever do is enough, that they can never please her. It is such a contrast for these men to go from work where they feel competent and effective, to home where they feel like no matter how hard they try they can never get it right.

These men often feel that their partners are constantly evaluating them and are angry at them all the time. The word I hear most often from these men is "criticized." Believing you are being criticized can become such a conditioned response. There are times when I sit with couples and a man says that he feels criticized and I can clearly see how his partner has just been critical. There are other times when a man says he feel criticized, and if I work hard to see things from his point of view I can kind of get how he might have heard what she said was critical, but it certainly was not my initial take on it. It's clear in those moments that I'm missing some of the man's early history or some part of the couple's history together that would help me understand why this sounds critical to him.

Tim is a young man in his late twenties who is in his first serious relationship with Nancy. Ever since Nancy moved in, it seems to Tim that their relationship has changed a lot, and not to his liking. It almost feels like Nancy has taken over his apartment, like she has a hidden playbook somewhere that he can't get access to. That playbook is filled with the details of how things are supposed to be done—the right way to load and unload the dishwasher, how to clean the tub after you take a shower, what gets washed with what and at what temperature, and so on. All of these things seem a little silly to Tim; after all, he managed just fine on his own for years. Still, it is nice to step into a clean tub for a shower or to see the unwrinkled clothes that she has folded and put away in the drawer. Tim is also surprised at how good it feels to have something concrete to do that is so pleasing to Nancy. However, over time, what started out feeling like not much to ask for begins to feel increasingly burdensome and resentful. Each time Tim starts to feel like he's got it, he's mastered the playbook and knows what's expected of him, damn it if she doesn't come up with another rule that, somehow, he was supposed to already know about. Sometimes it almost seems like a rigged game, that no matter how hard he tries he will never get it right, never be able to please Nancy. Curiously, the one thing that almost never occurs to Tim is to tell Nancy that he feels pressured not to disappoint her, and that he has some ideas of his own about how to run their shared home.

When a woman does not get the emotional responsiveness she is looking for from her partner, playing the role of his mother is an increasingly unsatisfying trade. Whether she works outside the home or not, in most families it is the woman who is in charge of the home and the family. She is the one who organizes, makes all the plans, and delegates responsibility for everything connected to the children, the running of the household, and all social relationships. Women get varying degrees of help when they ask for it. Some partners are quite compliant and eager to please, but women's frustration is that the responsibility for everything falls to them. They know damn well that their partner is competent and effective at work, so why the hell does he not see that the floor needs cleaning or even know where the mop is? As things deteriorate, these women increasingly see their partners as incompetent and believe that if they don't take care of things, or closely supervise their partners, the work either won't get done or won't get done correctly.

When things go badly in this way, the downward cycle gets worse and worse. As women feel increasingly alone, they express their frustrations in one of two ways. Some women escalate their demands as a way of expressing their resentment, which inevitably leads to more conflict and increased emotional distance in the couple. If she cannot get the closeness she wants, at least she can make his life as miserable as hers, and maybe get the garbage taken out without always having to nag about it as well. Although this strategy is rarely effective, sometimes the emotional distance in a relationship can be so severe that a negative connection can feel better than no connection at all. The second strategy women use is to withdraw, either as a way of punishing their partner for not stepping up, or as the result of giving up hope that they will ever find a way to get what they want from their partner.

Men express their dissatisfactions in one of three ways. Some men get increasingly angry with what feels unfair to them, leading to an increase in conflict. Other men are more passive aggressive, forgetting to do things they agreed to do, or doing them so ineptly that their wives are bound to be frustrated enough to just do it themselves, which also leads to a lot of conflict. When men come to believe that the situation is hopeless, that they will never be able to please their partners or bring the criticism to an end, the third way that men express their dissatisfaction is to begin to withdraw in a variety of ways. When this happens, their partner gets even less of what she wants, which leads to escalating demands and criticism on her part, and further withdrawal on his part, and they're off to the races.

As you might expect, sexual intimacy suffers in these couples. Men are not interested in being intimate because they feel under the gun, criticized, and judged, which can make them feel like they would be having sex with their mother. Women are not interested in sexual intimacy because they are tired of being rebuffed in their multiple approaches for emotional intimacy or even just their requests to get the garbage taken out consistently. The bottom line is that for most people, sex with someone who feels like their mother or their child is simply not very appealing.

Each member of these couples is absolutely convinced that they are the ones who have it worse and that the other is much better off, but this is a mess that they made together. The parent-child relationship is an unconscious collusion between two people. They are equally responsible and equally stuck. Interestingly, it is quite common to find these same dynamics in same-sex relationships, which suggests that this is more about power and gender socialization in our culture than any inherent difference between men and women.

The Truth Behind Every Fear

There is always some truth behind every perception, no matter how distorted or exaggerated it may look from the outside. Most people's fears are not imaginary, but rather an exaggeration or an overgeneralization of experiences that have been legitimately frightening. For example, people who are afraid of dogs have most often had some kind of bad experience with a dog in their lives. Even with people who are psychotic and clinically paranoid, there is almost always some grain of truth in even their delusional fears. In this case, we cannot really understand men's fears of women without making a good faith effort to understand the grain of truth that lies behind men's fears of being dominated and controlled by women. At the same time, it is critically important not to conflate the reality of those fears with the distorted claims of groups like the Men's Rights movement that paint men as victims and women as persecutors. As I stated in the introduction, there is no reasonable understanding of the world that rationally supports that conclusion.

In this case, there is no question that the large influx of women into the work force over the past decades has threatened what was men's unquestioned and unchallenged status and privilege, dramatically changing the relationship between male and female intimate partners. Men are rarely the "head of the household" in the way that their fathers or grandfathers may have been, although even in very traditional families there was some question about who actually ran the show. In the movie *My Big Fat Greek Wedding,* a daughter complains to her mother that she allows her partner to make all the decisions in the family. The mother replies, "the man is the head, but the woman is the neck, and she can turn the head any way she wants."[66]

There is actually a significant amount of evidence to substantiate men's belief that they are increasingly at risk for losing power in their intimate relationships. A 2008 study by the Pew Research Center study found that women make more of the decisions in most families than their male partners. Couples tend to share the decision-making in areas like deciding how to spend their free time or making large purchases. However, women are more likely to be the decision maker in financial matters, whether the woman works or not, or makes more or less money than her partner. Interestingly, couples over age 65 are twice as likely as younger couples to share the decision making equally, suggesting that having a more mutual relationship may be something that couples learn how to do over time, and that the younger generation may not be any better at it than the generations preceding them.

To go even farther down this road, new research suggests that women engage in significantly more controlling behaviors in heterosexual relationships than do their male partners, up to and including more frequent acts of both verbal and physical aggression.[67] In addition, men are less physically aggressive towards their female intimate partners than they are towards other men, whereas women are significantly more physically aggressive towards their intimate male partners than they are towards other women.[68] This suggests that men inhibit their aggression towards a female partner more than women do towards a male partner.

Let me offer two ways of understanding this troubling research. First, women's verbal and physical aggression in intimate relationships can be understood as another example of an oppressed group taking advantage of whatever covert power is available to them in intimate relationships that is not readily available to them either overtly in the family or in the larger world. Second, I think that women's aggression in relationships is often a response to their ongoing frustration at their inability to get the kind of meaningful connection with their partners they yearn for. In basketball, it is said that the ref always catches the second foul, meaning the first guy elbows the person guarding him, but the ref misses it, and when the second guy retaliates by also throwing an elbow, the ref sees that and calls a foul. Women, like the second player in basketball, are often the ones who get called for the foul because their partner's foul often goes unnoticed. On the simplest level, think about how you might respond if you are talking to someone who seems not to be listening to you. You would probably try talking louder to see if you can get their attention, and if that fails, and what you are talking about is important enough to you, you might even reach out and grab him.

The next escalation in fear for men is the progression from the fear of being dominated to the fear of being entrapped.

The preacher asked her
And she said I do
The preacher asked me
And she said yes, he does too
And the preacher said
I pronounce you 99 to life
Son she's no lady she's your wife

~~ Lyle Lovett *She's No Lady*

CHAPTER FOUR

MEN ARE AFRAID OF BEING ENTRAPPED BY WOMEN

The fear of being entrapped by a woman is another fear that is largely conscious for men, a fear that is socially acknowledged in the culture and something that men openly tease each other about and use as a measure of power and status in relationships among themselves. I use the term "entrapped," which is an active word that connotes someone else – in this case a woman – doing the trapping, rather than the more passive term "trapped." Men's obsession with not being controlled by women is the clearest indication of their fear of being controlled. A woman writer for the men's magazine *Muscle and Fitness* offered men ten signs that they might be "whipped."[69] Some of her signs are the kind of things that should be a legitimate concern for anyone in a relationship, like indications that your partner may be having an affair. However, some of what she suggests that men watch out for seem to advocate an almost paranoid, hypervigilance about any sign of "losing control" in a relationship. For example, she cautions men against allowing women to straighten their hair, make suggestions about clothing, or ask them to hold her purse while shopping. Again, we can see the underlying fear of being feminized in many of these cautions (see Chapter Nine).

Men's fears of being entrapped by women is frequently expressed in the fear of commitment in a relationship. The cultural stereotype is that marriage is an institution that benefits women but costs men, so that women try to entrap men into marriage and men try to stay single as long as possible, holding onto the freedom they believe women want to take away from them. A close friend of mine went to tell his father that he planned to marry his long-time sweetheart, and his father literally replied, "Son, marriage is an institution . . . If you want to spend the rest of your life in an institution, go ahead."

One person wrote about realizing that her partner's friends saw her as the obstacle to his happiness.

> *As a female partner of a man, I was the 'ball-and-chain', the nag, the brandisher of rolling pins in stern defiance of the pleasures of men. I was the obstacle that stood in the way of my boyfriend and the wonderful life that awaited him beyond the prison of my restrictive love. . .*

The 'man-cave' has been popularized as a much-needed space for men to take refuge from the stresses of women and married life. It is a safe place for men to do 'manly things' and escape the things that oppress them, like the presence of women, or shared responsibilities in the household. Women are not assigned caves, as marriage is known to be her refuge and the entire house her domain. Her husband, being neither tiresome nor shrill, is a welcome companion at all times. These stereotypes persist despite overwhelming evidence to the contrary. The data is quite clear that marriage serves men much more so than women in almost every way.[70] Married men are better off than single men; they are healthier, wealthier, and happier. Single women, however, are better off than married women. Married men are happier than married women, and unmarried women are happier than unmarried men.[71,72,73] Divorced men and married women have the highest rates of suicide.[74,75]

The only way marriage serves women is financially. Men and women's financial status tends to improve when they marry, but men's financial status tends to remain relatively unchanged following divorce, whereas women experience sizable drops in their household income, per capita income, and income-to-need ratios post-divorce. As a result, many women, especially mothers, fall into poverty following divorce.[76] Taken together, it looks like marriage is a system more designed to keep women entrapped in a marriage than men.

Despite the evidence, marriage initially seems like a good idea to most women. Two-thirds of college educated women in their twenties say they plan to marry, and women initiate two-thirds of the committed heterosexual relationships.[77] Men, on the other hand, often seem to be oblivious to the advantages bestowed on them by marriage and unaware of their own dependency needs that are most likely to drive them towards marriage. Two-thirds of college educated men in their twenties say they do not plan to marry, even though over eighty-percent of them eventually will.[78]

As economic conditions have changed, these dynamics also have change. Men traditionally could afford to delay marriage, knowing that they would likely have their pick of partners because men have traditionally married women who were less economically advantaged. As wealth is increasingly concentrated in an increasingly smaller group of people, and women's earning power grows, there are fewer men who have the financial resources to make themselves attractive as marriage partners. Accordingly, two-thirds of women without college degrees now say they do not plan to marry. Most people marry within their socioeconomic class. As blue-collar wages decline and unemployment increases, women have less incentive to marry for economic reasons.[79] Women considering marriage to blue collar men realize that it is unlikely that they will be able to stop working outside of the home, and yet will still be expected to do most if not all work in the house. Over time, more women come to understand that marriage is not such a good deal for them, and two-thirds of divorces are initiated by women.[80]

Dependency

"The original sin of 20th century men and woman is the sin of self-sufficiency."

~~ Rabbi Harold Kushner

"It is man's social nature which distinguishes him from the brute creation. If it is his privilege to be independent, it is equally his duty to be inter-dependent. Only an arrogant man will claim to be independent of everybody else and be self-contained."

~~ Mahatma Gandhi

The unconscious fear underlying the conscious fear of being entrapped is a fear of dependency. The fear of dependency in intimate relationships is where the dynamics of heterosexual and same-sex couples overlap. In Western culture, we tend to venerate independence to the point of self-reliance and look down on dependency as a dangerous vulnerability. We are the nation of great frontiers, which was built by those hearty souls who settled the west, self-reliant homesteaders who claimed a piece of land, built a cabin, and made their own way. We mark developmental milestones by the achievement of new levels of independence.[81]

Freud got the field off to the wrong start with his contention that individual needs are most important to people, and that relationships are a secondary means of either attaining or interfering with the satisfaction of those individual needs.[82] Psychological theories followed suit, conceptualizing individual development as a process of increasing separation and autonomy from the dependency of relationships.[83,84] While these values may be xenophobically taken as universal in the West, they are actually quite culturally relative. For example, Western cultures think of infants as helplessly dependent at birth and in need of training towards independence, but the Japanese see infants as independent at birth and in need of training towards mutual interdependency.

Similarly, we think of the emotionally mature person as someone who is intimate with others by choice but does not need anyone to be OK. Not surprisingly, in our culture, autonomy and independence are characterized as masculine qualities, while dependency is thought of as a feminine characteristic.[85] The stereotypes I described earlier about women trying to trap men into marriage stem from our tendency to attribute the desire for the inevitable mutual dependency of an intimate relationship to women, and to portray men as resistant to interdependency as a threat to the satisfaction of their own compartmentalized, individual needs.[86] In one study, men saw the potential danger of "entrapment or betrayal—being caught in a smothering relationship" in depictions of intimate situations on a projective test, whereas women saw danger in depictions of isolation.[87]

Men's underlying fears of being entrapped by women lead in large part to their adaption of the self-reliant and hypermasculine defenses that contribute to the epidemic of loneliness in men, men's impaired capacity for intimacy in relationships and the host of psychological and physiological issues we will take up more fully in Chapters Ten and Eleven.

Best selling author Ijeoma Oluo addressed men's unacknowledged dependency on women in a piece titled "Men, you can survive without us – please try."[88]

> *Men—straight, cisgender men. We need to talk. I've been concerned about you for quite some time. You've been acting out. The yelling, the name-calling, the violent outbursts—I've been watching with keen interest and I've finally understood the pain and fear at the root of it. And I need you to understand something: You can survive without us. Not only can you survive without us women, you can thrive. You can be successful, happy, fulfilled—all without us. Nobody likes rejection—it sure does sting. But you are so much more than your relationship to us.*

I know that you've been told that your identity is tied to being able to have sex with us, to provide for us, to keep us in close proximity to you at all times. And you're scared, because all that you've been told that you need for your manhood is at risk right now. We are refusing to have your babies, we are having babies without you. We are saying no to sex when we don't want it. We are earning our own money. We are running for president. . . But I'm here to tell you that you are so much more than that. You are so much more than your desire to catch and keep us. Your manhood will still stand if we refuse to sleep with you. Your days will still have purpose if you spend your evenings with friends instead of a wife. Your job will still be as fulfilling if the women in your life do not require your income to survive. Your buildings will not crumble if we are not stuck in your kitchens. You do not need our love if you love yourself.

"My mom said to me, 'You know sweetheart, one day you should settle down and marry a rich man,' and I said, 'Mom, I am a rich man.'"

~~ Cher

CHAPTER FIVE

MEN ARE AFRAID OF FAILING TO PROTECT AND PROVIDE FOR WOMEN

Stereotypically, protecting and providing for women and children is a large part of what defines masculinity. Men are expected not to need anything from anyone, while at the same time they are expected to make sure all their partner's and family's needs are seamlessly taken care of. A good man takes care of his wife and family, and if he falls short, he is judged by himself and others as less of a man. This is an obviously vulnerable position for men as they are continuously subject to failing and feeling bad about themselves.

The single biggest fear expressed in a survey of 5,000 men was that they would not be able to make their partner happy.[89] In fact, eight of men's top ten worries have to do with not being good enough for their partners or families. One man wrote about counsel he gave to a younger man.

> *I talked to a young man once who came to me for advice. He had saved up to buy his girlfriend a birthday present. It wasn't something expensive. He*

was 21 and just starting out in work life. His girlfriend scoffed at the present and told him she had hoped for something a little nicer. My advice, of course, was to get a better girlfriend or to do without . . . but he was unable to hear any of that. He just kept circling back to his dilemma that he wanted to please her but could not afford to do so. He even asked questions about career paths, with the inference being that he did not ever want to feel so inadequate again.[90]

Because these fears are largely internally and socioculturally generated, they are resistant to the point of being impervious to any interpersonal reassurance. It does not matter how many times a man's partner tells him how well her needs are being met, or how happy she is in the relationship. Men rarely feel they can relax the vigil of their fears, to escape the belief that they are "only as good as what they've done lately." This terrible sense of unending obligation and impending failure creates an enormous emotional burden for men and greatly impairs their capacity to experience pleasure, or even to know themselves separate from the needs of others. More on this in Chapter Ten.

These fears of disappointing their partners and families, along with their pathological self-reliance, stem from men's deep-seated beliefs that their needs don't really matter. This leads to a profoundly impaired ability to experience pleasure in almost any form. For example, Steve and his wife have both been working at home full time since the pandemic. His wife took the guest room for her office because her work required more privacy. Steve originally thought he was OK with that and was fine with using the dining room table for his work, despite experiencing the bulk of family interruptions because he was working in the more public space.

Gradually, Steve realized that he would like to move his office to a more private space and proposed to his wife that he set up shop in a large closet in one of the children's rooms. (There was actually a larger space available, but Steve could not even imagine bringing himself to ask for that more desirable space). Steve's wife told him that she did not like that plan, that it was not her preference, but that she understood how important it was to him to have a space of his own and that she was absolutely fine with proceeding. Steve was frozen. His wife repeated several times that she was *fine* with the plan, but as long as she didn't say she *liked* it, he couldn't get himself to feel OK about taking the space for his office. He said "I need her to want it too. . . I'm getting something I want, and I don't know if that's OK. It's not a right or wrong, which would be easier. It is harder to stand up for what I want just because I want it. She says what I feel is OK, but I won't believe it unless she feels that way too."

Will expressed similar sentiments about the family dog sleeping in the couples' bed. Will was uncomfortable sleeping in the bed with the dog but didn't feel entitled to move the dog out of the way and claim his own space. He lay in bed, night after night, hoping that his wife would move the dog, which is the only way it would be OK for him.

How do men get stuck in this role, which is so emotionally draining and creates so much resentment in their lives? First, men don't create this suffocating sense of obligation on their own. It is a folie à deux, as women have been socialized to expect to be taken care of by men as much as men are socialized to feel responsible for taking care of women. Unfortunately, women are also socialized to take care of men, in different ways. The end result in many heterosexual couples is that both people end up feeling stuck in the role of the caregiver, frustrated in their own and the couple's inability to work their way out of their polarized roles. They each feel obligated to take care of each other, but neither of them can really enjoy being taken care of because they are preoccupied with their potential failures as care givers.

Second, most men are still raised by women, most often their mothers, and their fathers are often emotionally less involved. As a result, men are more likely to feel closer to their mothers than to their fathers, and it is their mothers who teach them about emotions and relationships.[91] Many men have mothers who were chronically dissatisfied with the level of emotional closeness in their marriages. Frustrated in their attempts to get their partners to be more emotionally open and intimate with them, many mothers unconsciously recruit their sons to fill some of the emotional needs that are not being met in their marriages.[92] Freud based an entire psychology largely on the bind this creates for young men, what he called the Oedipal conflict, named after Sophocles' protagonist who unwittingly murders his father and marries his mother.[93]

Men's childhood experiences of feeling responsible for taking care of their mothers sets them up as adults to be hyper-focused on any indication that their partner is dissatisfied with them or just unhappy in any way. Research confirms that it is the woman's happiness that is the primary determinant of men's happiness in most heterosexual couples.[94] The childhood saying, "If Mamma ain't happy then nobody's happy" transforms into the new mantra of men's partnered adult life "Happy wife, happy life."

The problem is that young men inevitably fail at the job of taking care of their mothers because they don't have the adult resources or emotional maturity to meet an adult woman's needs. Men are hypervigilant for any sign that they are failing to please their adult partners because any hint that they are failing to take care of their families harkens back to their sense of having failed their mothers. They become obsessively focused on any sign of criticism, interpreting it as evidence of yet another need they have failed to meet, leading to a resigned sense of failure. Men in my office often complain that their partner has just said something critical, and I often have to strain to understand how they might have heard it that way. One man insisted that he could tell when his partner was upset as soon as he walked in the front door, before even seeing her. I don't doubt that they had become so mutually locked into these polarized caretaking roles that he could.

Taking care of women is a more conscious defense against two other more powerful unconscious fears that men have, the fears of being inadequate or abandoned, which we will address in Chapters Seven and Eight.

Men are afraid of feeling physically and financially responsible for women.

On the simplest level, men are socialized to feel physically and financially responsible for women, to protect them from harm, and provide for their physical needs. Everyday examples include men doing the yard work and repairs around the house and earning enough money so that their partner "doesn't have to work" and their kids can "have whatever they need." Most often it is the man in a heterosexual couple who gets up in the middle of the night whenever something needs to be investigated or taken care of, unless the children are the reason for getting up, because the children are women's responsibility.[95]

Taking care of their partners helps men feel good about themselves. Acts of service are the love language[96] that men are most familiar and comfortable with. Men feel good about themselves when they are able to take care of their partners successfully because they've been taught that this is an important part of their job as the man in the relationship. For most men, this is one of the primary ways they saw their dad express his love to their mom. Taking care of their partners also gives men enhanced status with other men. Men judge each other by the extent they provide for their family's physical needs and desires. When a woman shows up with a new car, that reflects positively on the man.

One of the primary ways in which men are taught to feel responsible for women is financially. This is a somewhat dated idea, but men still worry that women evaluate potential partners in large part on the basis of whether they will be a "good provider." Women will forgive a man a surprising number of faults, but he is generally expected to provide. Men feel this pressure from their partner's expectations about income and lifestyle, and the culture's evaluation of him by how well he provides.

Similarly, men can also be threatened by their partner's professional accomplishments and capabilities. As women gradually break through at least some of the glass ceilings, men are confused and threatened by their loss of unchallenged privilege in the workplace. Women understand this and are taught to dumb themselves down, that if they let men know how smart they are it will scare them off. The old saying "men don't make passes at girls who wear glasses," is a statement about men's fears of women being smarter than they are rather than a fashion caution.

This is a bit of a double bind for men because, although they may be married to smart, competent women who are quite capable of doing their part to support the family financially, men are expected, and expect themselves, to carry the burden alone. It is a sign of status for a man to say that his partner "doesn't have to work," meaning that he provides adequately for the family and does not need anyone's help. Men's anxieties about losing their protective privilege and being professionally or financially surpassed are justifiably intensifying. Women understand this and know that to be too successful risks being perceived by their partner not as a helpful reduction in financial pressure, but as a threat.

Many years ago, when my children were young, I came home from a weekend retreat at which my colleagues and I talked in depth about money and work-life balance. I asked my children how they would feel if I were to work more, be home less often, and earn more money. They looked at me like that was the stupidest question they ever heard. Why in the world would any child want their father home less often? I realized in that moment that the burden I had been operating under to "be a good provider" was largely of my own creation. Although I told myself that I was working so hard for them, they were largely oblivious and couldn't care less. I don't think my kids would have liked it if I quit my job and we lost the house, but my powerful drive to be successful was more about my fear of disappointing them than any expectation on their part.

Thirty years later and I haven't changed nearly as much as I would hope in this regard. I talk a lot about reducing the size of my practice and working less (he says in the midst of writing a 50,000-word book in his "time off"), but somehow, I get nervous that my perfectly capable partner who has a Ph.D. of her own, has authored nine books, and earns a very comfortable income somehow won't be able to take care of us, or at least, take care of us as well as I do. I also realize that my anxiety actually has little to do with money. If we had all the money we could ever need in the bank, there would still be a part of me that would feel a little guilty about working less, like I was not doing my fair share, not helping people I could help (it's only a few extra hours!), and letting my family down.

Men are afraid of feeling emotionally responsible for women.

Men are also socialized to take emotional responsibility for women, so much so that men often evaluate potential life partners based primarily on how much emotional caretaking they will require, with the ideal partner being described as "low maintenance."

One of men's most persistent complaints about women is that they are "too needy." On the simplest level, this complaint is an expression of men's resentment at being stuck in the seemingly endless and most often thankless role of being an emotional caretaker, a job that is not enjoyable for most men because it seems never ending and they don't feel very competent at it.

Going a level deeper, men's complaints about women being too needy also reflect the gender role expectations for men to be independent to the point of self-reliance, to not need anything from anyone, and to disdain dependency as a sign of weakness and vulnerability. From this perspective, relying on others is a luxury, a dangerous over-extension from the safe base of self-reliance. As is often the case in this culture, we tend to label values we don't respect as feminine and consider values to admire as male. In this case, men are raised to aspire to independence, often to the point of being emotionally self-reliant, and taught that to allow themselves to have needs that would lead to depending on others is less masculine.[97]

Men often complain about never being able to "ever get it right," meaning that no matter how hard they try to soothe any signs of discontent in their partner she "keeps moving the goal posts." For men, this is a game they can't afford to lose but can't seem to win. If it's their job to take care of their partners, then any sign of emotional distress means they are failing at their most important job. Men are perpetually looking for some sense of reassurance from their partner that they have been judged as adequate in their response to her emotional distress and that things can return to normal.

A woman simply being kind goes a long way with most men, and any withdrawal of approval or affection impacts men more strongly than they care to admit. Women implicitly understand this and are socialized to use withdrawing approval or the expression of emotional distress as an effective way to get the kind of emotional attention and connection from their partners that is often difficult to get any other way. Men implicitly understand that women can use expressions of emotional distress to balance the playing field by pressuring men to be better at attending to their partner's emotional needs. Accordingly, men often resent and resist being leveraged in this way, and respond by trying to minimize the reality of their partner's emotional needs or look for superficial "fixes" which will soothe their partner's distress and reestablish the status quo. Paradoxically, these efforts to suppress their partner's expression of emotion are, of course, incredibly unsatisfying to their partners and inevitably lead to an exacerbation, rather than a diminishing of what she's feeling. We'll take this up in greater detail in Chapter Eleven.

Men's criticism, if not disdain, for neediness can be very confusing because it's not like they want their partners to not need them at all. Men start to feel very insecure if their partners don't seem to need them at all. Men want their partners to need them enough to keep them from feeling insecure, but not need them so much that they start to feel disempowered and inadequate. Of course, women are taught to study their partners carefully (as all disempowered people learn to do with those in positions to hurt them) so that they can figure out where this sweet spot is and stay within it without any guidance from their partners who probably won't talk about it.

At the deepest level, men also work hard to soothe any sign of emotional despair in their partners because they are threatened by the level of emotion that is elicited in themselves in response to their partners feelings, an issue developed more fully in the next chapter.

Notes

As I saw it, all my mother's life, my father held
her down, like lead strapped to her ankles.

She was buoyant by nature; she wanted to
travel, go to the theater, go to museums.

What he wanted was to lie on the couch with
the Times over his face, so that death, when
it came, wouldn't seem a significant change.

~~ Louise Glück, Ararat

Chapter Six

Men Are Afraid of Women's Emotions

Men typically get very uncomfortable whenever women have strong feelings. This is particularly true when women are upset in some way, but men can also feel uncomfortable when women are excited, full of joy, or even really turned on. I remember the weekly dances in college where the women moved with grace, fluidity, and uninhibited eroticism that I yearned to join but that greatly intimidated me. Women understand this and learned long ago to suppress their own excitement in order not to make men uncomfortable.

Men are particularly uncomfortable whenever their partners are feeling anxious or distressed. It does not even have to be about them. Women can reassure their male partners endlessly that they are just upset, not upset with him, but that makes little to no difference. Men still feel compelled to curtail the expression of these emotions in their partners.

Why is an openly emotional woman so destabilizing for many men? Why don't men just ignore her and go off and do their own thing until she's over it? Why do so many men find women's emotions impossible to ignore? As with most things having to do with relationships, the answer is complex and multi-layered.

On the simplest level, as discussed in the previous chapter, men are raised to feel responsible for women's happiness. If their partner is unhappy, men believe they have failed in some critically important way.

Men are also less familiar with and less able to talk about their own feelings, so they feel disadvantaged when the conversation with their partner becomes more emotional. This is something like an American traveling abroad who wants other people to speak to them in English, rather than trying to learn at least some rudiments of the language spoken in the country they are visiting. Men are generally less emotionally fluent than their female partners because our culture stereotypically considers the world of emotions to be feminine territory. From early childhood, men are often derided or mocked for showing any sign of emotions other than anger (the one emotion allowed to men). "Big boys don't cry." "Don't be a sissy."

Men are also averse to their partners' strong feelings because they know from painful experience that emotions are contagious. Being around other people who are having strong feelings is as contagious as a yawn. When women are more emotional, men are likely to feel the internal stirrings of some of their own feelings that they are uncomfortable with and have learned to suppress. For men, being in an intimate relationship with a woman can be like being in alcohol recovery and hanging out with your friends at a bar.

On some level, men recognize that they are not as emotionally well developed as their partners. Women seem to have stronger emotions, have an easier time expressing their feelings, and are more empathic in responding to other people's feelings. Research does generally confirm that women are more emotionally expressive than men across a range of emotions and across numerous cultural settings,[98] although not nearly the magnitude of differences as hyped in books like *Men are From Mars.*[99] These differences in expression of emotion between men and women are not innate; they are largely taught.[100] Girls are socialized, primarily by their parents, at ages as young as four months old to be more emotionally expressive, while boys are often subtly conditioned to suppress any displays of emotion.[101]

On a more unconscious level, many men are scared that there is something wrong with them when it comes to emotions. Men worry that they do not have the kinds of feelings they should have—the kinds of emotions they see their partners expressing. My father died when I was a young man. I loved my father and was very close to him, so I decided I wanted to give his eulogy. My biggest fear was not that I wouldn't be able to get through it, but that I would not cry, which would confirm my worst fear about myself, that I was a cold, heartless son-of-a-bitch. I sobbed so much during the eulogy that the rabbi repeatedly tried to pull me away from the lectern. Although distraught, I also felt an enormous sense of relief. Interestingly, Freud theorized that when little girls saw their brother's or father's penis they would feel penis envy and judge themselves to be inadequate. On the other hand, little boys witness their mothers' and sisters' open display of emotions a lot more than little girls see a penis—thank goodness—yet it does not seem to have occurred to Freud that those boys might feel emotional envy and judge themselves to be emotionally inadequate.

Paradoxically, men also worry that if they ever were to give full rein to their feelings that could be dangerous. Women tend to suppress their emotions because they are afraid that if they open the spigot, they will never be able to shut them off. Men, on the other hand, tend to worry that if they relax their guard and give in to what they are feeling, the murderous rage they feel could get out of control and result in violence.

Consequently, men work hard to manage women's emotional experience in the service of protecting themselves from the discomfort—or even danger—of their own feelings. When a man's partner is upset, that becomes the single preoccupation in his life, as if nothing can happen until this situation is resolved. "If Mamma ain't happy then nobody's happy." This is not a process that men are conscious of, they are just aware of getting increasingly uncomfortable and feeling an urgent need to do whatever they have to do to get it to stop.

Anxiety is perhaps the best example of how these dynamics work in heterosexual relationships.[(1)] Anxiety in its simplest form is simply a preoccupation with a series of fearful predictions about an imagined future. Anxiety is not only normal, it is, to an extent, adaptive, alerting us to potential dangers.

In our culture, women tend to be more anxious than men.[102] Men hold more privilege, so things in general work better for them. Men face less challenge, less struggle, and less uncertainty in their lives than women do, so they have less to be anxious about. Women are biologically tied to their offspring, are at more risk of abandonment than their male partners, earn 30% less, and are more likely to live in poverty if divorced. Women feeling more anxious is just a realistic assessment of their situation.

In intimate relationships, women do far more than their share of the worrying. While men "help" in the family to varying degrees, it is primarily women who carry the load of tracking things and worrying about everything that needs to be done to run the family. Men typically don't even see this, and they get angry because, according to their calculations, the workload is about even, so they don't understand why it seems so unfair to their partners. One patient told me that he works about sixty hours a week and that his wife works about forty hours a week in her job, plus another twenty hours a week helping everything run smoothly at home and with their children. This seems like a fair division to him, and he has difficulty understanding why his sixty is not equivalent to his wife's forty plus twenty. I asked him if he would trade with his wife, cut back twenty hours a week at work and spend that time running the family. The look on his face made it clear that he got it.

Women, in turn, are socialized to be more openly anxious with their male partners because this is often one of the few effective ways of getting their partners to respond to their emotional needs. This often results in a mutually dissatisfying polarization in heterosexual couples in which the woman takes on the role of the anxious person and the man the role of the person responsible for managing his partner's anxiety.

Women understandably want to share the load. They want men to feel some of the anxiety they have been carrying as they have been protecting men from feeling their own anxiety. Anxiety is almost palpable and can be transferred from person to person in relationships. When one person feels anxious in a relationship, there is a natural desire to get someone else to take it off their hands so that they will feel less anxious. For example, one person in a couple might wake up in the middle of the night, feeling anxious and not able to get back to sleep. She wakes her partner and talks to him about what she's feeling anxious about, whereupon she goes right back to sleep, and now he feels her anxiety and can't go back to sleep.[103]

Men are particularly resistant to feeling anxiety themselves because anxiety brings with it a sense of passivity and powerlessness, a sense of being vulnerable and weak, in a one-down position, experiences that men are taught to disdain as not masculine. For men, being around women who are anxious puts them more in touch with their own disowned anxiety, which their privilege has largely protected them from experiencing. Men are taught to channel the expression of all their emotions into anger, an emotion that is socially acceptable to men because it feels more powerful and in control. As a result, men do their best to "take care" of women and "solve" women's anxiety to protect themselves from feeling more anxious.

---

(1) I'm describing anxiety as a feeling because that is how most people think of it. In fact, anxiety is more accurately conceptualized as what people often experience when internal conflicts interfere with their knowing what they are actually feeling, sometimes referred to as a secondary emotion. It is more of a prelude to emotion, rather than emotion itself. For example, if a woman is feeling angry at her partner, but historically it has not gone well for her in the relationship when she has expressed anger to him, she may experience anxiety and maybe be unaware of the anger that underlies her anxiety.

Notes

Men know that women are an overmatch for them, and therefore they choose the weakest or most ignorant. If they did not think so, they never could be afraid of women knowing as much as themselves.

~~ Samuel Johnson

CHAPTER SEVEN

MEN ARE AFRAID OF BEING INADEQUATE

Now we move into the three primarily unconscious fears that underlie all of men's other fears of women: the fear of being inadequate, which this chapter focuses on; the fear of being abandoned; and the fear of being feminine. The latter two are discussed in the next two chapters. All of these are the deeper fears that underlie the more conscious fears we have discussed to this point.

Men are socialized to equate masculinity with self-confidence, to put up a good front and always present as self-assured, even when they are not. "Never let them see you sweat." Men are trained to think of life as a zero-sum game, with winners and losers, so they attack any indication of a fear of inadequacy in another man as a sign of a weakness that can be exploited. As a result, men's fears of being inadequate go underground, hidden from themselves, and from other men.

Men's Fears of Being Interpersonally Inadequate

In early childhood, boys and girls typically play together. It is only later that they separate by genders, with the girls playing with other girls, and boys playing with boys. Girls focus primarily on relationships, playing house or school and with dolls, practicing skills that will help them to excel in relationships. Boys, in contrast, play sports and other games that focus on individual achievement and competition, practicing the skills that will help them in the hyper-competitive world they are headed to.[104]

The transition to same-sex peer groups is a part of a larger transition for boys which involves relinquishing the warm, tender world of intimate relationships represented by their mother to pursue access to the power and privilege in the world outside of the family represented by their father. Attractive as the world of their father is, this transition means giving up the intimate friendships of their youth to enter the hypercompetitive non-relational world of men. Boys' early friendships are as intimate, and as important to them, as the friendships that girls have, and giving them up to pursue external success has a tremendous cost that endures into their lives as men.[105]

I have only been arrested once in my life. When I was sixteen years old my best friend and I went out for the evening. When I drove him home, I parked in the middle of the dead-end street next to his house, thinking I would only be there for a minute. We started talking in the emotionally intense kind of way that young men can talk with each other as they explore the kind of relationship depth that is possible between two people making their way through the challenging life transition of coming of age. Lost in our conversation, I eventually shut off the engine to save gas. Several hours later, a police car pulled up behind us, lights flashing, and took us into the station, despite the fact that we were parked directly next to my friend's house. To this day I have no idea what the charges were, but I've always thought that there was something about the appearance of shared intimacy that was unsettling to that cop.

As puberty arrives, boys and girls get interested in each other again. This creates a conflict for both boys and girls; how to approach the other gender to get these newly emerging sexual and relational needs met without giving up the values of their same sex peer groups. Boys are immediately at a disadvantage in this coming back together of the sexes, and they know it. While the girls have been practicing, almost rehearsing, for this moment for years, the boys have not been giving it much thought, much less preparing. One woman told me that she spent hours as a little girl practicing kissing the back of her hand, teaching herself how to kiss her imagined future partner. This new game is played entirely on the girls' well practiced relational turf, where the boys feel unprepared and inadequate.

I learned a lot about gender roles in relationships from our male rabbit named Fez. Rabbits are happiest as pair-bonded animals, so after five years as a bachelor we decided to get Fez a female partner. After trying Fez with several available ladies, he and a younger rabbit named Mila seemed to hit it off. Mila had been raised in the shelter with other rabbits, so she had a lot more experience in relationships than Fez. Mila immediately began approaching Fez and initiating courting behaviors, which essentially meant that she pushed her head under Fez's chin and waited for him to groom her. Poor Fez was clueless. He had no idea of what was expected of him, and he basically just froze. Mila didn't waste much time expressing her desires. As soon as it was clear that Fez wasn't going to respond, she bit him, and little bits of fur went flying in the air. It went on like this for a few days. Fez gradually got the message, and began grooming Mila whenever she approached him, eventually even initiating the grooming himself and receiving grooming from her. Once Mila taught Fez how to be her partner, everything was fine. They lay together, cuddling in the sunlight for hours on end, happily mated for years.

A lot of women reading this are probably shaking their heads and identifying with Mila, resenting all the hard work they've had to do to train up their partners and teach them how to be in a relationship. At the same time, a lot of men are probably identifying with poor Fez, remembering all the times their partner "bit" them for not knowing what the hell they were supposed to be doing. Like poor Fez, men often feel clueless and terrified that their interpersonal inadequacies will be exposed. Things tend to go well in these new relationships as long as men take a clue from Fez and humbly turn to their new partner to help them get up to speed. Things don't go nearly as well when men, out of fear, are not open to new learning and default to the aggressive and competitive skills that got them there. More on this in Chapter Eleven.

Men's Fears of Being Sexually Inadequate

"I want you to want me.
I need you to need me"

~~ Cheap Trick, *I Want You to Want Me*

It is not surprising that heterosexual men's fears of inadequacy show up most clearly in the intimate setting of the bedroom. Fears of erectile dysfunction are only the tip of the iceberg. Men's fears of being sexually inadequate run all the way from the depths of questions about their manhood to fears about whether they can ever be loved.

Men have always seen themselves as vulnerable, even helpless at times, to resist women's sexual allure. Adam, Samson, Ulysses, and many other heroes were destroyed by their lust for women. Research substantiates that men think about sex more than women do, they are more interested in having sex with a wider variety of partners, and they seek and initiate more sex.[106]

While many of the sexual norms related to gender roles in our culture have changed dramatically in the past few generations, one norm that stubbornly resists change is the one-sided expectation that men should be the pursuers in heterosexual relationships. With rare exception (dating sites like Bumble), a man is expected to be the one to approach a woman to ask her out, make the arrangements for the first date without knowing much of anything about who she is or what she might like, and to be the initiator of most, if not all, sexual activity between them. Incredibly, this last expectation endures for the entire length of the relationship for most heterosexual couples, regardless of how sexually enlightened they may consider themselves to be in other areas of their relationship. One man said, "There's a process that happens with me with women. I see a woman I find attractive, I feel attraction, (and then) it quickly goes to desire and need, and I worry that I will be insufficient. And it happens just like that (snaps fingers). I've been struggling with that for years. I'm afraid of a woman's power, but that's really power because of my need."

Women have to live with the anxiety and frustration of waiting to be approached and suffer with all of the body image and self-esteem issues that come with being relegated to the passive position of being the object of men's desires. Men have to live with all the fears of being rejected because they are socialized to believe that a woman will reject them if she is "out of his league," i.e., higher status than he is. One man said "When I go on dates, I am usually anxious and can't wait to have a couple of drinks and I relax. The more I idealize women (good looking, sexy, etc.) the more I am made anxious by them and afraid of them." In this way, when men approach a woman, they are risking not just the one rejection, but facing an entire evaluation of their worth as a human being.

Assuming they make it past the early stages of dating, men then have to face all of their fears about pleasing women sexually. It all starts with basic anatomy. Men have external genitalia and cannot hide when they are sexually aroused and when they are not, which leaves them exposed to shame and ridicule. Men are taught that they must be sexually aroused to pleasure their partner and to propagate. While their partners can have multiple orgasms (but how many is enough?) and are ready to continue intercourse immediately after an orgasm, men generally have only one orgasm at a time and have to wait to be ready again.

Approaching a woman openly with their sexual desires is an inherently vulnerable act for men that often stirs up deep seated fears of inadequacy. Much of what young men learn today about sex comes from watching pornography, which creates a confusing set of conflicting expectations for them. On one hand, the women they are dating likely make it clear that what they are looking for in relationships is mutual, emotional openness and vulnerability. This directly contradicts what young men are learning from watching pornography or talking to their friends. We equate masculinity with a sexual desire so strong as to be indiscriminate, that a real man is eager for sex anytime, anywhere, and with anyone.[107] There is an urban myth that men think about sex every seven seconds, which would equate to 8,200 times every waking day. As it turns out, men actually think about sex more like once a day, less than they think about food and sleep.[108]

One ninth grader said that from porn he learned that "guys need to be buff and dominant in bed, doing things like flipping girls over on their stomach during sex. Girls moan a lot and are pretty much turned on by everything a confident guy does." One particular porn scene stuck with him: "A woman was bored by a man who approached sex gently but became ecstatic with a far more aggressive guy." Another fifteen-year-old, who had never had sex, said that watching porn gave him performance anxiety. "You are looking at an adult. The guys are built and dominant and have a big penis, and they last a long time. And if you don't do it like the guys in porn, you fear she's not going to like you."[109] When you add to all this the anxieties and confusion resultant from what young men see in the news about the "me too" movement, they may be left completely confused about what level of sexual assertion will attract and satisfy a partner but is not a transgression.

To make matters even more confusing, women themselves often carry the same split between what they want from a man in their emotional relationship versus what they have been socialized to want from men in their sexual relationship. A popular dating website published a list of the "Ten most dangerous mistakes men make with women." The number one mistake they claim men make is "Being too much of a nice guy."[110] Women's erotica is sometimes referred to as "bodice rippers." It is all about being taken, ravaged. Boys learn that girls are interested in being friends with you if you are a nice guy, but they are more sexually drawn to the bad boys.

Men are stereotypically thought to be narcissistic and self-centered lovers, focused primarily on their own pleasure and largely uninterested in their partners' experience, except as an instrument for their own gratification.[111] One man told me that he thought of sex as "masturbation with a woman in the general vicinity." In contrast, when surveyed, men said that satisfying their partner was more important to them than their own pleasure, and that what turned them on the most was depictions of intense sexual pleasure in women.[112] Men's pornography reflects this powerful need to please in its images of women who are overcome with desire in response to their male partners expert ministrations. How can men be self-centered lovers interested only in their own pleasure and simultaneously be more focused on their partner's pleasure than their own? The paradox is readily resolved with the understanding that men's focus on their partners' pleasure is only partially an act of generosity, and primarily an effort to stave off their own feelings of insecurity.

One of the reasons that sex is so important to men is that the homophobic prohibitions against men touching each other in any kind of intimate way mean that sex is often the only opportunity men have to intimately touch and be touched by another person. A member of a men's therapy group recently said that for many years he looked forward to coming to the group every week because the hugs the men exchanged afterward were the only time he could count on touching and being touched all week. Men—particularly, but not exclusively, single men—can go days, weeks, months, or even years without any kind of intimate touch in their lives.

Men's sense of sexual urgency runs much deeper than just a need to be touched. There is an old saying that women need to feel loved to want to have sex, and that men need to have sex to feel loved. Feeling an almost desperate need for the masculine affirmation that comes with sexually pleasing their partners creates a deep vulnerability for men. Sometimes the physical intimacy of sex is the only way that men can feel truly loved, but seeking that reassurance requires men to be vulnerable in ways that evoke their deepest fears of abandonment.

Women are often confused by their partners' sense of urgency about sex, mistakenly attributing those reactions to misguided notions about the strength of men's libido. We similarly misunderstand men remarrying quickly after divorce as a reflection of those same urgent needs. It is not that men's sexual appetites are inexhaustible, it's that their need for reassurance about their fears of abandonment run that deep.

Men's requests for more sexual frequency are often similarly misattributed to male libido. If it were that simple, men who are partnered would simply masturbate more often when their partner is not interested or not available. What women often don't understand is that when they are more open about their own sexual desires, this frees men from the insecurity they feel about being rejected, or more profoundly, from feeling not desirable or even not lovable. Men often feel like they are putting their entire sense of worth and self-acceptance on the line when they approach their partners sexually. Intercourse for men is a literal return to the insides of a woman's body, the place from whence they came, so it is a powerfully regressive experience, the ultimate reassurance of their acceptance, and a symbolical test of their self-worth.

Women's orgasms are critically important to men for similar reasons. Men report feeling more masculine when their partner has an orgasm.[113] The more insecure a man feels about his masculinity, the more important it is to him that his partner have an orgasm. Women understand this and so have been known to fake orgasms to reassure their partners. One woman said, "If he doesn't think I had an orgasm, he won't give up, just keeps at me until I feel pressured."[114] It's clear that this kind of pressure is about more than generosity on the man's part. It is also a reflection of men's need to prove themselves to be adequate, worthy of being loved, and to forestall their fears of being abandoned.

As you would expect, men's fears of being sexually inadequate have a significant effect on their relationships with their partners. Noted sex therapist Esther Perel says that men's reliance on sex to reassure themselves about their larger sense of adequacy leads them to be so other-centered in sex that they are afraid that if they truly inhabit their bodies and surrender to the experience of their own pleasure for just a moment, their partner will be hurt or angry, and will punish or even abandon them.[115] As a result, sexuality for men is often filled with more anxiety than pleasure, more focused on performance and pleasing their partner, and their own pleasure is often overlooked. Men often approach women in a way that doesn't say 'I want you' as much as 'Do you want me?'[116] Men are being careful, which is what they think they are supposed to do, but taken to extremes, this can be a turn off for women, more like a little boy asking for permission than a man expressing his desire for them.

This is why men's sexual fantasies are often about women who are ravenous in their sexual desire. It is not just about power and control, it is also about anxiety. In these fantasies, the women's clear desire relieves men of worrying about whether their partners want them, or if they will offend a woman with their own sexual desire. These fantasies allow men to set loose their own repressed sexual desire, to focus on their own pleasure without risk of being rejected.

Paradoxically, when women meet men's fantasies by being more open about their sexual desires, men often experience women's open expression of desire as a demand rather than an invitation, a command to perform, to please her. History is full of examples of men viewing women's sexuality as dangerous. Delilah brought down Sampson by seducing him, the Sirens brought Odysseus to near ruin with their seductive cries, Eve brought about humanity's fall by seducing Adam to eat the apple. As I've mentioned, even today, athletes are superstitious about having sex before a big match believing it drains some of the power they need to perform. To protect themselves, men have historically instituted systemic ways of suppressing and controlling women's dangerous sexuality, ranging from requiring women to sit in a walled off section of the sanctuary in places of worship to not distract men with their sexual appeal, to requiring women to wear burkas, veils, or other clothing to hide their bodies or hair, to surgically removing women's clitoris to prevent her from experiencing sexual pleasure.

Not surprisingly, these dynamics often show up as inhibited sexual desire in men. In one study, fifteen-percent of men in long-term partnerships reported they had lost almost all interest in sex for a period of three months or longer in the past year. This is not about aging, because the highest rate was in men aged 35 to 44.[117]

Somehow, we have managed to create a dynamic in which both men and women feel terribly anxious, deeply unsure of themselves, and cut off from their own sense of pleasure. They feel disempowered. The best we have been able to do is cobble together a narrative in which men are the sexual initiators in order to reassure them that they are in control, while women demur in order not to intimidate men with any open display of sexual desire. But then the women need to succumb to men's approaches, which reassures men of their adequacy and gives women permission to surrender to their own sexual desire.

Notes

I've always been scared of women.

~~ Cary Grant

CHAPTER EIGHT

MEN ARE AFRAID OF BEING ABANDONED BY WOMEN

Now we get to the heart of the matter, the two unconscious fears that largely drive the more conscious fears that men have of women: the fear that they will be abandoned and the fear of being feminine. This chapter deals with the abandonment fear, while Chapter Nine will address the fear of being feminine.

Human infants are far more dependent on their caregivers, usually female, for a longer period of time than other mammals because our brains are bigger and we have to be born before we are fully developed so that our heads will fit through the birth canal.[118] Most mammals can get around and eat on their own from birth, tasks that take human offspring months or years to accomplish. Psychologically, human infants are just as dependent on their caregivers. Infants are born undifferentiated from their caretakers, meaning that they literally do not understand that they exist as a person separate from their caretakers.[119]

To understand the emotional power of this early attachment, remember the "Still Face" experiment mentioned at the start of this book.[120] That kind of symbiotic attachment is not easy to separate from, but children need to separate emotionally from their caregivers in order to form other attachments, first with peers, and then eventually with a romantic partner.

This process of separation from one's earliest caregiver is more complex and conflictual for boys than it is for girls. Girls are not expected to make a complete break from their mother. In our culture it is perfectly acceptable for women to remain close to their mothers, and this is generally not seen as an obstacle to establishing a romantic relationship with a partner. Women can maintain a strong emotional connection with their mothers and supplement that with a new, hopefully even more intimate, emotional connection with a partner. No one looks askance at an adult woman cuddling in bed with her mother to watch a movie during a visit home or seeing a mother brush her adult daughter's hair.

Unlike girls, boys are expected to relinquish their strong attachment to their mother in order to mature into young men. When a man remains close with his mother, we do think of that as a potential impediment to an adult intimate relationship with a woman. Men need to relinquish their intensely intimate connection with their mother in order to form an intimate romantic relationship with a woman, i.e., you have to get out of bed with your mother in order to get fully in bed with a woman. Accordingly, many people would be critical of a man cuddling in bed with his mother to watch a movie on a visit home. This is one of the reasons that all cultures have prohibitions against incest, to forbid the enactment of those powerful feelings and help people move on to more mature relationships with an adult partner. Ideally, this is where first a male caregiver and then close male friends come in, helping young men transition to the world of men.

The transition to adulthood does not always go well for young men. For one thing, it requires that the primary caregiver have adult attachments that are satisfying enough to compensate her for relinquishing the all-consuming connection she has shared with her children. Even under the best of circumstances, the transition involves significant loss for both the mother and child and leaves all of us with some residual anxiety about separation and abandonment. This anxiety can range from the kind of separation anxiety you see in couples who are threatened by their partner's increasing individuation, to the kind of fears of abandonment that are strong enough to sabotage an intimate relationship.

Men sometimes resolve this conflict by creating an internal split between intimacy and eroticism, sometimes known as the Madonna-Whore complex[121]. In this split, men are able to have an emotionally intimate relationship with a partner that replicates the closeness they felt with their mothers. However, they cannot allow themselves to have sexual feelings for their partners because that would feel incestuous. They split off those erotic feelings and transfer them to another woman (real or imagined) with whom they can be sexually aroused but not intimate. Splitting off their erotic feelings to another woman protects men against the full strength of their fears of being abandoned by "not putting all of their eggs into one basket." At the same time, this creates a profound dilemma for many men in which they are sexually uninterested in any woman they love and unable to love any women they are sexually interested in.

Men's Fears of Conflict in Intimate Relationships

Men's fears of abandonment in relationships are perhaps most visible in the lengths that men will go to avoid conflict in their relationships. Men monitor their partners' emotional states constantly and carefully, scanning for any signs of potential conflict, criticism, or disapproval. Any evidence of unhappiness or disapproval is often interpreted by men as criticism or failure. They immediately assume they have done something wrong, that they are "in the doghouse," and will not return to favor until they figure out what they have done wrong and correct it. Reassurance from their wives that they are not "in trouble" is rarely sufficient for men to feel off the hook.

Men are often willing to contort themselves to almost any extent to avoid having a woman be angry with them. It is not uncommon for men to become so conflict avoidant in their intimate relationships that placating their partners becomes their *raison d'être*, the most important thing in the relationship to them. Here, again, the "If Mamma ain't happy then nobody's happy" mantra of their childhood is replaced by "Happy wife, happy life." Men can become so unsettled by their partners being angry or disapproving of them that nothing else matters until that is fixed. All they want now is for her to stop being mad at them.

Why does it seem so urgent for men to avoid conflict? If men are the ones in the privileged position, conflict should be to their advantage and they should be able to count on winning most of the time. Interestingly, men are so much more comfortable with conflict in other settings that they often seek it out. Corporate work environments have often been compared to a kind of civilized combat, with all sorts of ritualized avenues for the expression of aggression and conflict. When a sports team is in a prolonged slump, the players often call a players-only meeting in which they "clear the air," meaning come clean with each other about the anger and resentments they've been holding.

Men are more comfortable with conflict in business and sports because conflict in those settings is all about defeating your opponent and winning. The only risk is that you might lose the conflict. Men aren't afraid of losing an argument with their partners. They are afraid of losing the emotional reassurance and validation that their partner has been providing so seamlessly for so long that they are largely unaware of it until it is threatened. They are afraid of losing the validation their partners provide by listening to their stories about work, laughing when they are trying to be funny, exaggerating their sexual pleasure during lovemaking, and a thousand other forms of reassurance. Men try to withdraw into self-sufficiency to protect themselves against the power of these vulnerable needs, but the threat of their partners withdrawing affection evokes the earliest fears of childhood emotional abandonment.

Sometimes men try using the same tactics they use successfully in business and sports to help them manage the vulnerability of conflict in their intimate relationships, with predictably disastrous results. My mother was an attorney, and I was raised in a family in which conflict was a blood sport. Anything was fair game, and arguments were hyper-rational and aggressive. Not knowing any better, I carried those same strategies over into my former marriage. I argued like a lawyer, presenting my positions logically and rationally, looking for openings to attack any flaws in the logic of my opponent, my former wife. Eventually, I wore my wife down and finally "won" an argument. I persisted until I "broke her down," and she collapsed into tears. I was horrified. Not only was I not enjoying any of the ecstasy of victory, I felt absolutely horrible about myself for the way I had treated someone I loved. Trying to defeat your life partner in an argument is like trying to use your army to enforce democracy in another country. Even if you win, you now have to occupy that country indefinitely to enforce your will because they didn't ask for your help to begin with and probably didn't want it.

Changes in divorce laws have also made men even more conflict avoidant in their relationships. Divorce used to be something that men did to women, something women worried about. Men did not have to worry about their wives filing for divorce unless they were caught cheating. Men generally remarry much faster than women, and they don't suffer as much financially in a divorce, although if they have been the primary wage earner they often think of the money in the family as belonging to them and resent having to share it with their ex-wife who "didn't earn it." More recently, as men have become more involved as fathers, they have more to lose in a divorce and worry more about their partners leaving them. Men now often stay in bad marriages longer than women because they are afraid of being estranged from their children, and fathers often have less contact with their children after divorce.[122]

Over time, men can get so gun shy about conflict in their relationships that they just stop trying. When men talk to me about the aspects of their marriages in which they are unhappy, I ask if they have ever talked to their partners about any of what they are telling me? Typically, they look at me as if I were crazy. How could I not understand that talking to their partners about any of this would just make things worse?

Nothing makes men more anxious than for a woman to be masculine.

~~ Gloria Steinem

Chapter Nine

Men Are Afraid of Being Feminine

Femiphobia is the fear of being seen as feminine by others or by oneself. It is distinguished from gynophobia, which is the fear of women.[123] Femiphobia is the largely unconscious fear that underlies all of men's fears of women.

On the simplest level, men are afraid of being seen as feminine because anything feminine is devalued in our culture. Any man showing characteristics that the culture associates with femininity suffers a decrease in power and status, such as gay men, any man not comfortable being aggressive or competitive, men who are not interested in sports, and particularly men who allow themselves to be controlled or dominated by women. Men accuse each other of being more feminine in order to secure their own place in the pecking order of masculinity: sissy, pussy, mamma's boy, wimp, pansy, letting the woman wear the pants in the family, don't throw like a girl, and so on. The only lower status for a man than allowing himself to be controlled by a woman is a man who allows himself to be used as a woman by other men. In prisons and any other setting in which women are not available for sex, having sex with another man does not lower your status if you are the penetrator, only if you allow yourself to be penetrated like a woman.

Beyond the loss of power and status, men are afraid of appearing feminine to themselves or others because their maturation into manhood requires not only that they embrace the world of men, but also that they forgo the world of women. The transition to manhood requires young men not only to separate from the most tender intimate relationship they have ever known, but also to publicly and internally repudiate their mothers along with any trace characteristics that the culture considers feminine. This includes forsaking the intimacy they have shared with other male friends, along with characteristics such as warmth, tenderness, empathy, compassion or being emotionally open or vulnerable with someone. In the same ways that the Jim Crow laws in the South exposed the fears of the privileged caste as they categorized people as Black if they had "one drop of African blood,"[124] our culture's insistence on the total repudiation of anything considered the least bit feminine in men similarly exposes just how scared men are of women.

Most preindustrial cultures have a ritual to mark a boy's transition to manhood. Prior to initiation, boys often live with their mothers in the women's quarters. The ritual generally begins with the men symbolically kidnapping the boy from the women's custody and removing him from the community for a period of time. That the removal requires a symbolic kidnapping is a recognition of the boys' ambivalence about leaving their mothers. When the boy returns, he reenters the community as a man. In one particular ritual, the boy's mother greets him when he returns, and the boy slaps her in the face before gathering his belongings and moving into the men's quarters. We might ask ourselves, why does the ritual require the young man to slap his mother when he returns? Why not just pick up his belongings and move in with the men? The slap is intended, in part, to assert the boy's newfound status as a man to his mother, but perhaps the young man also slaps his mother to demonstrate his repudiation of his mother and any connection to the feminine she represents to the other men.

The repudiation of the feminine as a requirement for masculinity means that masculinity is a culturally shaped construct that is defined more by what it is not (feminine) than on any developed understanding of what it is: a flight from the feminine, sometimes known as "fragile masculinity." Anything that is defined primarily by what it is not is necessarily less well developed, less mature, and more fragile. For example, many young men are primarily determined to be nothing like the man their father was, which makes it all the more difficult to discern the man they truly are.

Femininity in our culture is a birthright, something that young women inherit simply by virtue of being female, whereas masculinity is something that young men are taught they have to earn and then is subject to being challenged at any time and must be defended at a moment's notice. It has been said that "womanhood happens to girls, via a series of inevitable physical and biological changes." In contrast, "Real manhood . . . is not a natural condition that comes about spontaneously through biological nature but rather is a precarious or artificial state that boys must win against powerful odds."[125] The rituals that mark young men's transition to manhood often involve the administration of intense physical pain, sometimes to the point of torture such as scarification or circumcision without anesthetic.[126] Although many cultures have corresponding rituals of passage for young women, "an authentic femininity rarely involves tests or proofs of action, or confrontations with dangerous foes."[127]

A single (i.e., feminine) act can undo a lifetime of hard work. Boys are taught to feel uncertain and insecure about their masculinity, to feel that it is fragile and vulnerable, and that they need to suppress any feminine aspect of themselves to continually prove to themselves and others that they are a man. When a group of college students at two universities were asked how a man might lose his manhood, they answered with a series of social failures such as losing their job. When asked how a woman might lose her womanhood, the same students gave biological explanations, such as having a sex change operation or a hysterectomy.[128] Boys are punished more than girls for deviating from socialized gender norms.[129] For example, parents tend to be less worried about their daughter being too masculine if she plays with a truck than they are worried that their son is too feminine if he wants to play with dolls.[130]

Men protect themselves by being hypervigilant about anything that might make them appear feminine and doing all they can to appear more manly, from what they wear, to how they hold their bodies, how they talk, eat, and the like. This leads to a "chronic terror of emasculation"[131] for men, and the use of hypermasculine defenses that we will take up in more detail in Chapter Twelve. Men's devaluing of the feminine is a projection of their own femiphobia, a defense to protect their own fragile masculinity. What men experience as a fear of women is actually a projection of their femiphobia.

Much of men's suffering comes from this alienation from the parts of themselves they have been socialized to think of as feminine. Men are socialized to suppress stereotypically feminine qualities such as compassion, empathy, nurturance, tenderness, vulnerability, and intimacy and only allow themselves to explore those aspects of themselves in private intimate relationships with women. Men are frightened of women because women embody those feminine traits and threaten to reconnect men with the parts of themselves they are fleeing, or worse yet, to publicly expose those parts of themselves. As a result, men can be tender and snuggle and use pet names privately but are mortified if their partner reveals any of that outside the relationship, particularly to another man, because they would be seen as feminine.

Section III

The Impact of Men's Fears of Women

In this section, we will look more closely at how men's fears of women impact the lives of individual men, and their intimate relationships with women. The first chapter describes the concept of Gender Role Conflict in men, and elucidates the defense mechanisms men most often utilize to cope with their fears of women. The second chapter takes up some of the broader sociocultural effect of men's fears of women in intimate relationships, including hypermasculine defenses utilized by men and Intimate Partner Violence. The chapter concludes with an examination of the role of men's fears of women in the political system of the United States.

Only grown-up men are scared of women.

~~ Ernet Lehman

CHAPTER TEN

THE IMPACT OF MEN'S FEARS ON INDIVIDUAL MEN

On the simplest level, men's fragile masculinity and the repudiation of the feminine that the culture requires leaves them less able to be fully themselves. As a result, men are dissociated from the more emotional, tender, compassionate aspects of themselves, and impaired in their ability to be vulnerable and intimate with other men, with women, and with their children. Jung[132] and other theorists[133] defined emotional well-being as the capacity to integrate, to fully embrace all aspects of experience. For example, the capacity to feel happy when you are happy, sad when you are sad, angry when you are angry, and scared when you are scared.

It follows that blocks in our capacity for experience are what create less than optimal wellness. This may play out as someone with a restricted capacity to grieve when experiencing a significant loss, or to feel joy when something special happens, or to feel angry when someone tries to hurt him, or a restricted capacity to feel scared in the face of danger. People stereotypically think someone is depressed when they feel very sad. From this perspective, feeling sad means you are not depressed, particularly if you have good reason to feel sad. Depression is not feeling too sad, but a restricted capacity to feel sad. Depression is emotional constipation, not emotional diarrhea.[134]

Gender Role Conflict

Gender is one of the earliest and strongest forms of individual identity.[135] People are more likely to group others on the basis of gender than race, age, or social role.[136] Parents start differentially reinforcing their sons and daughters as early as four months of age, cultivating emotional expression in their daughters while teaching their sons to hide any evidence of emotion. Boys and girls make distinctions based on gender in infancy.[137] Children at an early age hold gender-based beliefs about what boys and girls like to do.[138] That early socialization is highly resistant to extinction, meaning that it's a lot harder to unlearn than it was to learn.[139,140] As boys mature and gravitate towards playing with other boys, their newly important friends strongly reinforce these rigid gender expectations, and boys become increasingly verbally and even physically abusive towards other boys who deviate from the accepted gender roles.[141] We know that most of this gender socialization is learned rather than innate because children taught in an intentionally gender-neutral environment have many fewer gender-based biases.[142]

Masculinity is a social construct, what one author called "a collective hallucination . . . a reality that seems to be found everywhere but is actually nowhere to be 'found' that can be summarized as the expectation that "means being in control, having mastery over yourself and the world around you. It means taking charge . . . The desire for power and control is at the heart of most of our notions of masculinity."[143] Some of the all-too-well known gender-laden expectations of boys and men include:

- success is a measure of manhood. Men have to achieve to feel good about themselves as men;
- men always have to be in control to feel secure;
- men can never fail;
- men can never show weakness or they risk being taken advantage of;
- men are less masculine if they do not take care of their families;
- emotions are not masculine, and being vulnerable and emotionally open is dangerous;
- men are self-reliant and never need help.

As discussed in the previous chapter, men are punished more than girls and women for deviating from socially accepted gender norms.[144] Because masculinity is a social construct that can never be fully achieved, men suffer from a chronic lack of confidence and self-confidence about their masculinity. Men's inevitable failures to meet these socialized gender-laden expectations create Gender Role Conflict, or "GRC."[145] Deviation from these gender role expectations leads to a loss of stature or devaluation by others, and internal conflicts about being weak, less of a man, or worth less than other more gender conforming men. This can be conceptualized as internalized oppression, the process in which oppressed people come to see themselves through the eyes of the system that is oppressing them. In this case, men fear becoming the feminized person they worry others might see them as. For example, a boy blushes with embarrassment when his mother gives him a kiss on the cheek in front of his friends, worried that his blush will reveal the longings for closeness that he still has, and fears that his friends will mock him for being too feminine. That boy grows to be a man who is a rising young executive in a cut-throat corporate environment who suppresses the distress he feels in response to his colleagues' ruthless approach to eliminating their competition. He knows that his colleagues will mock him for the same reasons his friends did when he was a little boy. Gender Role Conflicts are an expression of men's underlying femiphobia, their fears about having any thoughts, behaviors, or emotions that are associated with the feminine.

A gay man told me that he spent his childhood feeling like an outsider with his nose pressed up against the glass, watching the straight boys at least act like they knew how to be accepted as masculine. He described the tremendous sense of relief when he learned later in life that the straight boys felt as much outside of masculine acceptance as he did. Looking back, he realizes that there is no one on the inside with a secure sense of masculinity, there are just people who have gotten good at pretending.

Men respond to these Gender Role Conflicts by either restricting how they show up in the external world, or more insidiously, restricting who they allow themselves to be. Symptoms of GRC tend to show up in four areas: success/power/competition issues; conflicts between work and family issues; restrictive emotionality; and restrictive affectionate behavior between men. Much like Jack's[146] groundbreaking work on women silencing themselves in relationships in response to restrictive gender roles, there are almost one-hundred studies linking GRC in men with a variety of problems.

More than thirty studies have linked high GRC with depression in men.[147] Low self-esteem and suicide are also correlated with high GRC.[148] More than thirty studies have linked high GRC with anxiety and stress. GRC is also linked to risk-taking behaviors and negative attitudes towards seeking help. Men with the strongest beliefs about masculinity were only half as likely as men with more moderate masculine beliefs to get preventive health care[149], including mental health care,[150] and the more men conformed to masculine norms, the more likely they were to engage in heavy drinking and tobacco use.[151] For example, men who are financially dependent on their wives engage in more unhealthy behaviors and die younger.[152] Men who are secondary earners for long periods of time experience poorer physical health and are at increased risk of cardiometabolic diseases (e.g., diabetes, heart problems, high cholesterol, hypertension, and stroke) and stress-related issues (e.g., back problems, chronic lung disease, psychiatric problems, and stomach ulcers). High GRC is also linked to high blood pressure and to substance use and abuse.

GRC also strongly effects how men are in intimate relationships. High GRC is negatively related to intimacy in relationships and positively related to low relationship satisfaction and happiness. Twenty-five studies found a link between high GRC and negative attitudes towards women and gay men. High GRC is also correlated with hostility and aggression towards women, and delinquent and abusive behavior towards women.[153]

Gender Role Conflict tends to be fairly consistent throughout men's lifespans.[154] Restricted emotionality remains the most consistent conflict over time, but older men tend to be less conflicted about the masculine expectations around competition and striving for success and power than younger men. GRC is higher in men with lower socioeconomic status and less education.[155]

Fear and Defense Mechanisms

In this culture we tend to label emotions as "positive" or "negative," with fear being one of the emotions that is most often labeled as negative. Fear itself is not negative or positive. Fear has no value other than the judgments we impose on it. Fear can be adaptive. There are things in life we have good reasons to be frightened of. Being afraid of things that pose a legitimate threat to us is highly adaptive, and there are negative consequences for those who ignore this adaptive fear. Wearing a mask and social distancing to avoid being infected with a virus is a great example.

There are other things that people become frightened of that are less likely to be a threat to their physical or emotional well-being. This typically happens when people experience harm in one situation and then over-generalize that fear to all similar situations. For example, a man who is hurt by a bad breakup in a relationship may over generalize to a fear of being abandoned in future relationships.

Just because the experience of being scared is not by itself harmful, that doesn't make it particularly pleasant to experience. People in general, and men in particular, are aversive to experiencing fear and will go to great lengths to avoid it. Fear itself, whether in response to a realistic assessment of a threat or an over generalization from a prior harmful experience, limits our capacity to be fully ourselves. When we are scared our bodies tense, they tighten up. The same thing happens in the psyche when we are scared. We tighten up, restrict, and become less fully ourselves.

Psychological defense mechanisms are strategies we use to protect ourselves from experiencing emotions that are uncomfortable or even threatening. They are a way of pushing uncomfortable feelings out of our conscious awareness. The problem with defense mechanisms is that they work, but they are a double-edged sword. Defense mechanisms are effective in protecting us from feeling scared, but they protect us by tamping down our capacity to feel, which restricts our capacity to be fully ourselves or to be intimate with others.[156] Over time, the defense mechanisms we use to avoid feeling scared become more of a problem than whatever it was we were originally scared of. As Franklin D. Roosevelt famously said during the depths of the Depression, "The only thing we have to fear is fear itself." For example, someone who is afraid of snakes may adapt the defense mechanism of avoiding situations where there might be snakes. While this strategy might well serve to protect them from seeing a snake, clearly that avoidance has the potential to be more limiting in that person's life than the original fear of snakes. For men, the defense mechanisms they use to protect themselves against experiencing their fears of women can become more of a problem than the fear itself ever was. In fact, it is the hypermasculine defenses men use to protect themselves against experiencing their fears of women that are the cause of most of men's bad behavior towards women.

One of the simplest psychological defenses is avoidance, in which one simply avoids exposure to uncomfortable feelings.[157] Examples of an avoidant defense men use to protect themselves against their fear of women is avoiding intimate relationships with women all together or allowing themselves to be in relationships with women but being careful to limit the emotional depth of the relationship in order to avoid feeling their fears.

When men do cautiously allow themselves to be in an intimate relationship with a woman, and then despite their best efforts the depth of emotional connection between them begins to deepen, men may then turn to another common defense mechanism, which is denial. Denial serves to block any awareness of uncomfortable or prohibited feelings. Most men are in denial of their fears of women, but the awareness of those fears does not lie very far beneath the surface. If you ask a man if he is afraid of his partner, he will almost certainly get defensive and claim that is not true. However, it doesn't take long for most men to recognize those fears within themselves. The simple act of a man moving through that initial denial and recognizing his own fear is often the beginning of a transformative process.

Another way that men experience denial concerns how emotionally dependent they are on their partners. Having been strongly socialized to be emotionally independent to the point of self-reliance, it is anathema to men to think that they need their partners. This is why I recommend what I call the "Mrs. Piggle Wiggle cure" for most young couples.[158] *Mrs. Piggle Wiggle* is a series of children's books in which the protagonist prescribes odd exercises for children and families to help them recognize and correct bad behavior. My Mrs. Piggle intervention for men who are in denial of their dependency is to have their partners book at least a long weekend, and preferably a full week out of town. I ask the men to take whatever time off from work they need to take care of the home and family, and not to use their resources to bring in help such as nannies or sitters, mothers-in-law, or prepared food. While this intervention only addresses men's denial about their physical dependency on their partners and not their even more extensive emotional dependency, it is a start, and with any luck, will generalize to more learning.

Another common defense mechanism men use to protect against knowing their own fears is called reaction formation,[159] which means to act in a way that is the opposite of what you feel in order to avoid experiencing the feeling. For example, men who are afraid of being controlled and dominated by women, or afraid of being entrapped by women, often protect themselves against awareness of that fear by trying to be as physically and emotionally self-reliant as possible, in order to avoid any kind of dependency on their partner. Men who are afraid of women's emotions often protect themselves by working to be hyper-rational and suppressing their own feelings, hiding them from their partners. Men who are afraid of feeling inadequate often pump themselves up with narcissistic or even grandiose and entitled defenses. Men who are afraid of being abandoned often try to limit the extent they allow themselves to care about their partner in a prophylactic effort to minimize the potential damage. Finally, men who are afraid of being feminized often adapt hyper-masculine defenses to deny their hidden underlying fears.

A less common defense mechanism is called a counter-phobic defense.[160] In avoidant and denial defenses the person seeks to avoid all exposure to situations that cause him distress. In a counter-phobic defense, the person actively seeks out the situation that is causing him distress in hopes of overcoming that distress. For every fear there is an accompanying, often hidden or denied pleasure. The counter-phobic defense against the fear of being dominated and controlled by women is to embrace the fear and seek out situations in which you can indulge in the pleasure of being dominated by a woman. Because being dominated is so forbidden, embracing the feeling of being dominated can take on a powerful erotic charge. One way of enacting this defense is for a man to engage as a submissive with a partner who is dominant. This is sometimes done with the help of a professional dominatrix, a woman who is paid to engage in BDSM (bondage, discipline, and sadomasochism). Professional dominatrix practice is open and legal in many states because there is, by agreement, no sexual contact. The sole purpose of the relationship is for the man to be able to surrender to the pleasure inherent in allowing himself to be dominated.[161]

A final defense mechanism regularly used by men whenever they have more of an emotional reaction in a relationship than they are comfortable with is the defense of intellectualization. Men often adapt a hyper-rational defense whenever they feel threatened by emotional dysregulation in a conflict with an intimate partner. They withdraw emotionally from any investment in the argument or, in extreme cases, withdraw emotionally from any investment in the relationship.

This is emotional withdrawal is often effective in preventing men from feeling emotionally flooded with their partner, but like all defenses, it is a double-edged sword. As we will discuss in more detail in the next chapter, when men utilize a hyper-rational defense and emotionally withdraw from engagement with their partner, this generally results in their partners pushing even harder for the emotional engagement that men are already trying to avoid. When their go-to hyper-rational defenses not only fail to soothe their own emotional dysregulation but actually result in an escalation of their own emotional distress, men often adapt an even more aggressive defensive strategy, seeking to actively suppress their partners' feelings that are causing them so much distress. They do this by claiming privileged access to a heretofore unknown rulebook for couple's conflicts that clearly stipulates that it is better to remain calm and rational in an argument than to become emotional and hysterical. In other words, the person who stays calm and rational wins.

When all is said and done, all the defenses that men use to protect themselves against feeling their fears of women end up either escalating how scared they feel, or leaving them feeling unexpectedly, and very uncomfortably, alone.

The Pandemic of Men's Loneliness

One of the most pervasive and debilitating costs of men's fears of women in relationships is the epidemic of loneliness in men today. It could be argued that for men, loneliness is the disease of our age and a direct outcome of our rigid gender role expectations of men.[162] Thomas Joiner in his ground-breaking book *Lonely at the Top*[163] says that men have made a Dorian Gray-like trade of success in the external world for a deep sense of loneliness, emptiness, and disconnection. Boys start out feeling just as connected in their close friendships as girls do, but they tend to neglect their personal relationships to pursue external success. When men lose the protective social structures provided in high school and college, they often find themselves interpersonally adrift, unsure how to establish or maintain close relationships with men or women.

In heterosexual couples, women tend to handle all the social relationships outside of the family, establishing and maintaining relationships for the couple and the children. This falls to women because they are aware that their male partners do not have substantial relationships outside of the family as they do. They pull their partners into socializing with other couples so that the women can have more time socializing with each other without that becoming an issue in the marriage. They may even arrange "play dates" with their friends' partners so that their partner will be more interested in socializing as a couple.

Women do this so seamlessly that their partners often remain blissfully unaware of all the work their partners are doing to manage the social relationships in the family. Men are happy to have their partners take care of this because they are socialized not to value social relationships very highly, and on some level, they may also recognize that they are not very good at it themselves.

When I work with men, I always ask them if they have any friends. Most men quickly reassure me (and themselves) that of course they have friends. Similarly, a reporter for *The Boston Globe* was initially offended when his editor asked him to write an article about "how middle-aged men have no friends."

> *Excuse me? I have plenty of friends. Are you calling me a loser? You are . . . I quickly took stock of my life to try to prove to myself that I was not, in fact, perfect for this story.*
>
> *First of all, there was my buddy Mark. We went to high school together, and I still talk to him all the time, and we hang out all the . . . Wait, how often do we actually hang out? Maybe four or five times a year? And then there was my other best friend from high school, Rory, and . . . I genuinely could not remember the last time I'd seen him. Had it already been a year? Entirely possible.*
>
> *There were all those other good friends who feel as if they're still in my lives (sic) because we keep tabs on one another on social media, but as I ran down the list of those, I'd consider real, true, lifelong friends, I realized that it had been years since I'd seen many of them, even decades for a few.*[164]

There are a few men who have already figured out that they don't have many friends, they don't like it, and are willing to talk about it. For the men who insist that they do have friends, I ask them if they talk with those friends about the kinds of things they talk with me about, and they almost always look either surprised, or worried that their therapist has asked such a stupid question. It is typically only when they are divorced or widowed that men realize how few relationships they actually have that have not been arranged or managed by their partner, and how vulnerable they have been in depending entirely on their partners for all of the connection in their lives.

Loneliness is not only an unpleasant feeling; it is an interpersonal impairment that causes significant harm in the lives of men. Research suggests that a focus on the accumulation of wealth and material goods results in less overall happiness in life and less satisfaction in intimate relationships.[165] The Harvard Study of Adult Development followed a group of men for eight decades.[166] Throughout the study, at different points in their lives the men were asked, "Who would you call in the middle of the night if you were sick or afraid?" Those men who had someone to turn to were happier in their lives and their marriages, and also physically healthier over time.

The danger here is not only the emotional cost of loneliness, although that is substantial. Close relationships with other people have more of an impact on our physical health and longevity than even our genes do.[167,168] A satisfying relationship life can extend longevity by up to twenty-two percent. Loneliness is a risk factor comparable to smoking, obesity, and high blood pressure.[169,170,171] Loneliness in men is correlated with cardiovascular disease and stroke. Eighty-percent of successful suicides are men, and one of the leading contributing factors is loneliness.[172] While many physicians ask questions about risk factors such as smoking and alcohol consumption during an annual physical, the research suggests they should also be asking about how satisfying their patient's closest relationships are.

Similarly, it is my experience that men are often profoundly impaired in their capacity to experience pleasure. They may engage aggressively in recreation, or frequently express interest in sex, or organize expensive adventure vacations, but when you dig a little deeper you often find that men have massive prohibitions against allowing themselves to experience any pleasure for its own sake. They are comfortable with pleasure when it is productive in some way, like playing golf with business associates to "work on their game," or being comfortable with pleasure only when it benefits other people, like vacations for the kids. However, pleasure for the sake of pleasure, that is not for someone else's benefit and not productive in any way is often a real challenge for men. We could think of Steve's difficulty feeling comfortable taking space in the family in Chapter Five as a profound impairment of his capacity to accept pleasure from his partner.

I have observed painfully in my own life that I am capable of turning any pleasure into an obligation. I got interested in golf and then played obsessively in order to get good enough not to be embarrassed when playing with other men, and with other women. I moved to a small island in Maine recently to slow down the pace of my life, and then somehow decided that this was the perfect time to finish this book. I loved being here on vacation in the summers because I would just sit on the porch and read for hours or spontaneously nap in the hammock in the middle of the day. Since I've moved here, and now work here, it's been much harder for me to allow myself those kind of self-indulgent pleasures for their own sake.

We turn now to a consideration of the impact of men's fears of women on couples, and on the culture at large.

Notes

Men marry women with the hope they will never change. Women marry men with the hope they will change. Invariably they are both disappointed.

~~ Albert Einstein

More women are becoming the men they wanted to marry, but too few men are becoming the women they wanted to marry. That leaves most women with two jobs, one outside the home and one inside it.

~~ Gloria Steinem

Chapter Eleven

The Impact of Men's Fears on Couples

Tom and Lisa are having an argument. Lisa is hurt and angry. Tom can clearly see that Lisa is upset, and her tears make him surprisingly uncomfortable. While Tom would like to feel more empathic, there is something about Lisa's strong feelings that is distressing to Tom and gets in the way. Because Tom is uncomfortable with his own strong feelings, he begins to emotionally withdraw and detach to protect himself. For reasons he doesn't fully understand, it becomes increasingly important to Tom to remain rational and unemotional, and he is increasingly critical of, and irritated with, Lisa for being "too emotional." Lisa can feel Tom withdrawing, and the more he withdraws, the more anxious Lisa becomes and the more urgently she pursues him, trying to find a way to make some kind of emotional connection with him. Now they are locked in a mutually destructive cycle; the more Lisa pushes for the emotional connection she yearns for, the more Tom detaches. The more Tom tries to control his own fear by detaching, the more anxious Lisa gets.

This argument may be painfully familiar to many of you. Rather than helping couples work through things and feel closer to each other, this is the kind of conflict that devolves into an increasingly destructive power struggle, with each member trying to "win" (whatever that would mean) rather than making a genuine effort to understand each other and work towards a mutually satisfactory outcome. Each member of the couple believes that he or she is doing their best to get to a better outcome, yet together they seem unable to avoid repeating that same unhappy ending, again and again. When this pattern repeats over years or even decades, couples can get to the place where they lose hope of ever being able to work things out between them.

Over time, most systems, including the intimate system of a relationship, tend to devolve towards increasing polarization of roles. Couples generally start with more idealistic aspirations about doing things differently than their parents did, but it's easy to slip into more traditional gender roles, both logistically and emotionally, because this is more efficient. When everyone knows what their job is, conflict is easier to avoid.

Women are drawn into the role of being the emotionally needy one who wants more intimacy in the relationship and is frequently disappointed in their partners. Women learn to settle for acts of service from their male partners as a not very satisfactory substitute for the emotional intimacy and closeness they desire, and they turn to their children and other women for the connection and intimacy they need. They settle, in part, because they are taught by their mothers and other women to protect themselves from repeated disappointment by significantly lowering their expectations of men. One woman said:

I want to talk about relationships or feelings more than my husband does. Over time, I have chosen not to bring up the topic of how I want more from him every time I feel it. I don't assume he is ready to talk, or that he should be ready to talk (the latter is harder). I do a lot of self-pacing and checking his facial expressions to see if he is open to me. I realize that means that I live with a situation where I get less than I want, but is there an option? He is my rock and a great husband and father in many ways that count for me. I do long for more of the good stuff than he is able to give. I would rather have a little that I cherish than to make a stink and still come up empty. (Re-reading this I realize Charlie would disagree with this last sentence. I make a protest regularly and pull on him to make time for us. But I try not to totally blow up the relationship and get enraged every time.)

Men are drawn into the role of the stoic unemotional ones who are a lot more interested in intimacy than they let themselves or their partners know about and are constantly frustrated at their inability to please their partners. They learn from their fathers to express caring and to be good men through acts of service. They feel good about themselves to the extent they are protective and helpful to the people they love, and they feel like failures when anyone in their family is upset and they can't fix it. It is not hard to see how this is often a volatile mix. This pattern is known as the "wife demands / husband withdraws" (WD/HW) pattern, which research shows is a powerful predictor of marital dissatisfaction and divorce.[173]

This rigid gender role arrangement, although stilted for both people, works well enough for some couples for years or even decades. It works as long as women feel loved by the acts of service their partners so eagerly provide, and as long as there is not enough conflict in the relationship to activate men's fears of being inadequate or abandoned. Couples unconsciously settle into a set of role expectations that enables each of them to both give and receive love and to feel good about themselves.

Over time, however, this increasingly rigid polarization of roles has an increasing cost. What started out as a satisfyingly symbiotic understanding can gradually degrade into a mutually frustrating arrangement in which both partners feel increasingly resentful, increasingly distant, and trapped. Each partner genuinely believes that they can no longer be themselves in their relationships, which is the most common explanation people give for divorcing, "I just didn't feel like I could be myself anymore."

For women, settling for acts of service starts to wear thin, or may even become annoying because it reminds them of what they are not getting. Women increasingly resent being the one in charge of everything in the family, including the relationship. Men are eager to please and happy to "help," but their baseline is "if it ain't broke don't fix it." Men are focused on avoiding conflict rather than aspiring to greater closeness, so their initiation of connection in the relationship is likely limited to sex. As a result, in most heterosexual relationships, the initial expression of dissatisfaction or unhappiness is most likely to surface with the woman first.

When women try to talk about their dissatisfactions with their partners, no matter how carefully they do it, their partners are likely to hear it as a criticism. Their fears of being controlled by a woman and of being inadequate for failing to take care of her cause men to experience their partners' overtures as demands. In response, men do what people typically do when they are scared: they withdraw. They respond by withholding some of their protective caretaking to punish their partners for not being appreciative and giving them the reassurance they crave. When women are rebuffed in their efforts to talk directly with their partner about their unhappiness, they resort to expressing their desire for more connection indirectly in ways that are more concrete and, they hope, less threatening. For example, women may object to their partner not spending enough time with the family rather than risk talking directly with him about missing him and wanting to feel closer. Women may complain about their partner always having to be asked to help around the house and with the kids and never pitching in on his own, rather than talking with him about the profound sense of loneliness she struggles with and her yearning to feel like she has a true partner.

While couples often get stuck arguing about these issues on a concrete behavioral level, in some ways, men do understand that the level of connection their partner is asking for is not only reasonable, it is something they privately yearn for themselves. However, men's fears of women make it difficult for them to hear their partners' approach as the invitation it is intended to be. Instead, it feels like one more in an endless series of criticisms and incessant reminders of their failures as a partner and as a man.

As men withdraw further, women get even less of what they want from the relationship, and their level of emotional distress increases. Strangely, this is often more satisfying for women than the indirect approach they have been using, at least initially. They fight more with their partners, but sometimes negative connection feels better than no connection at all. This is why couples who are divorcing continue to fight with each other long past the point it makes any financial sense to do. They are not yet ready to let go of each other, and fighting is the only connection they have left.

Then there is the problem of tolerance. Like any drug, over time you need more of the same drug to get the desired effect. Men continue to withdraw from their partners' emotional forays and become increasingly desensitized, so women have to escalate their level of emotion and threat to continue to get a response from their partners. The problem with using emotional distress to leverage connection is that the kind of connection women are able to get this way is not very satisfying. It certainly doesn't feel anything like what they were hoping for—not very authentic or mutual. When men don't understand why the kind of attention they are giving to their partners doesn't satisfy them, I ask if they ever had sex with someone who wasn't really "in the mood," which helps them understand something of their partners' experience.

Men feel emotionally triggered by their partners' escalating emotions in ways that feel out of control and very uncomfortable to the men. Their first line of defense is to treat their partners' expressions of emotions as if they are problems that need to be fixed, most often taking the form of reassuring their partner when she is upset and minimizing and explaining away her feelings. Leading with what they know, men offer heartfelt, well-intentioned "solutions" to their partner's distress and then are baffled, if not resentful, when their partner tells them they are not listening. Genuinely confused, men then repeat verbatim what their partner has just said, proving conclusively to their partner that, while he may have been listening, he did not hear her. It is terribly frustrating to women to realize that their partner is working hard to fix something that is obviously not the problem, and that he seems incapable of understanding what the problem really is.

It is terribly frustrating to men that all their efforts to lower the emotional temperature in the relationship only seem to raise the heat. The more controlled and stoic they become, the more emotional their partners get. The more they withdraw, the more she pursues. I have had a number of men tell me that, in a desperate attempt to get away from the emotional dysregulation they feel in an argument, they have literally locked themselves in another room, only to have their wives pursue, screaming at them and pounding on the door.

In a desperate attempt to reestablish control over their own emotional equilibrium, men respond by clamping down even tighter on their emotional responsiveness. They withdraw to their familiar fortress of solitude and do their best to convince their partner and themselves that they don't need her. This strategy allows men to maintain at least a superficial connection with their partners, which modulates their fear of being abandoned, while also modulating the level of their own emotional activation. Men's withdrawal precipitates a panic in women. Men are so good at presenting themselves as impervious and completely self-reliant that it is not clear to their partners how far they are willing and able to go in this emotional standoff.

In addition to using detachment in an effort to soothe themselves, men often try to shut off the problem at the source by actively suppressing their partner's level of emotional expression. They hold themselves up as the model for women to follow: logical, rational and most importantly, in control of their feelings. They may criticize their partner for being "too emotional," or shame her for being "hysterical" and "blowing things out of proportion." Men do everything they can to control the argument by keeping things on the turf where they feel comfortable and competent: sticking to the "facts," remaining rational, and keeping all feelings out of it. Men act as if a woman who is expressing emotion is drunk, and they are the self-appointed designated driver. The more she drinks, the more sober they are determined to be.

It is difficult for women to be understanding or to respond compassionately to their partners' emotional withdrawal because compassion requires an empathic understanding of another person's experience. Men aren't socialized to think much about their internal lives, so they typically don't know a lot about it, and they are not very practiced at communicating. Women are often left to conclude that the problem is that they are too needy and that their partner is either incapable or unwilling to give them what they want.

Experiencing themselves as having little overt power in the relationship, women resort to the only form of power that is safe for disempowered people, which is to claim their power subversively in private spaces where their partners are more vulnerable. There is an old story that enslaved people used to spit in their owner's soup right before serving it, a myth that was revived in the best-selling book *The Help.* In it, a woman horribly shames and humiliates her maid, who then makes the woman a “chocolate pie” that is actually full of her own feces.[174]

As women grow increasingly frustrated in their relationships, they begin unconsciously wielding the only subversive power they have by conditionally withholding some of the emotionally validating responses they understand their partners are highly dependent on. They provide less of the support, approval, validation, and reassurance that men don’t even realize they are dependent on until it is withheld.

In 2009, the retail business J. C. Penney ran an ad in which a man who gives his wife an insensitive gift for their anniversary is condemned to the purgatory of the “doghouse,” where he joins other men who are folding laundry in perpetuity, waiting for forgiveness from a tribunal of women who harshly judge their progress. Men tend to respond fairly concretely, working stubbornly to understand what they did wrong so they can fix it and get out of the doghouse and regain their partner’s approval. To men, being in the doghouse seems like a rigged game. They don’t understand the rules, or if there even are any rules. They correctly ascertain that no amount of the kind of concrete acts of caring that they are comfortable with will get them out of the doghouse of their partner’s disapproval.

Both partners are confused about how things have gotten so much worse. Each of them tends to see the increasing conflict and decreasing satisfaction in their relationship through the lens of their own experience, and neither of them understands enough about their partner’s internal experience to be able to make meaningful shifts in the dynamic.

A woman in her fourth year of marriage participated in a workshop I facilitated on men's fears of women. She wrote this about that experience:

> *As a woman who grew up with a lot of scary, angry men, it didn't dawn on me much that I had any impact at all on men, much less to be able to scare them. . . My marriage had been stable but difficult, frequented often by bouts of rage (mine) due to what I felt was my husband's unwillingness to hear me and see me or to take me seriously. Through the workshop I came to understand both my own rage as I heard it echoed in a variety of emotions and experiences of other women in feeling dismissed, hurt, ignored, not taken seriously, not stood up to by their partners, but even more profoundly, to understand that the men in the group were not ignoring, dismissing, or hurting their female partners on purpose or out of a lack of respect—as I suspected. Instead, they were scared. Scared to hurt us, to mess up with us, to not be enough. I had honestly never in my life heard men talk this way, to articulate that the women in their lives were so profoundly important to them that they were constantly terrified we'd leave them—a threat I often made in my rages, semi-seriously at times, assuming it had no impact.*

Men are socialized to express their caring through acts of service and to feel good about themselves when they succeed in satisfying their partner's needs, so naturally, they think the problem in the relationship is that their partners are too needy and can never be satisfied. Their partner's escalating requests seem increasingly critical, like an endless series of demands and underlying criticisms. It is distressing and unsettling to men when they do everything they can think of to soothe their partner yet she remains distressed and seemingly dissatisfied with him.

This is why men's dissatisfaction in relationships tends to be expressed as anger about being criticized and controlled while women's dissatisfaction tends to be expressed as disappointment in their partner's inability to get anything right. Men's jokes about women tend to be hostile expressions of their belief that their partners are preventing them from feeling good about themselves by being impossible to please. For example, "How did the medical community come up with the term 'PMS'? Mad Cow disease was already taken." Or "Is Google male or female? Female, because it doesn't let you finish a sentence before making a suggestion." Women's humor about men tends to express their disappointment in criticisms about men's ineptness around the home and in relationships. For example, "A man asks, 'God, why did you make woman so beautiful?' God responded, 'So you would love her.' The man asked, 'But God, why did you make her so dumb?' God replied, 'So she would love you.'

The Vietnam Syndrome was Richard Nixon's diagnosis for the malady he saw as enfeebling the American body politic. Its symptoms were shame and guilt about power, a reluctance to use it to 'defend national interests' and an unmanly predisposition towards compromise, negotiation, and the pursuit of common agreement.

~~ Stephen Ducat "The Wimp Factor."

CHAPTER TWELVE

THE SOCIOPOLITICAL IMPACT

A public health expert was once asked what the most dangerous things in the world are—AIDS? Guns? Mutating viruses? The expert said that was an easy question, that males aged 19 to 24 were by far the most dangerous force in the world.[175] Despite volumes of research attempting to blame male's bad behavior on biology, this chapter will consider men's socially aberrant behaviors as defense mechanisms against their internalized femiphobia.

The enormous pressure that all men in this culture experience to conform to a rigid set of gender-laden norms that are not an authentic expression of who they are leads to the development of a precarious or fragile masculinity, as was discussed in Chapter Nine.[176,177,178] The idea is that femininity is a given, a birthright, but masculinity is fragile. Masculinity has to be first earned, then defended. Masculinity is something you do, while femininity is just something you have. Men are expected to actively earn and maintain their status as "real men" or risk losing their privilege in their intimate relationships and their place in the world. Masculinity is tenuous. It can be taken away, or lost, and must always be defended and justified. One of the primary strategies that men utilize to protect their precarious sense of masculinity is the adoption of hypermasculine defenses.

Hypermasculine Defenses

In the face of what men often experience as threats to their identity as a man, they often resort to hypermasculine defenses, adopting postures sufficiently masculine to prevent anyone—even oneself—from questioning one's masculinity. There is a scene in the movie "Planes, Trains and Automobiles,"[179] in which two men who are traveling together are forced to share a bed for the night. They wake up having unconsciously snuggled next to each other. They leap out of bed in a homophobic panic and immediately adopt self-reassuring hypermasculine poses, with one of them asking "How 'bout them Bears this year?"[180]

The magnitude of any psychological defense reflects the degree of insecurity of the person using the defense. The more extreme hypermasculine defenses men adopt, the less secure they are about their masculinity. For example, men who scored higher on a scale measuring homophobia showed more sexual arousal when exposed to homoerotic images than less homophobic men.[181]

Here is a partial listing of some of the more common hypermasculine defenses and their consequences:

- A singular obsession with success as the sole measure of masculinity, which can lead to workaholism, the neglect of family and any other personal relationships, and impaired capacity for pleasure in any form.

- Self-reliance, which can result in the inability to delegate or function effectively as a part of an efficient team, and a difficulty being sufficiently emotionally vulnerable to get close to anyone.
- Emotional constriction and the belief that letting anyone know how you feel is a dangerous vulnerability, which can lead to a profound sense of loneliness.
- A narrow-minded focus on strength to the extent that many men cannot acknowledge to themselves or others when they need help with something. This leads to men avoiding preventive care and developing much higher incidence of illnesses thought to be related to stress. Men with the strongest beliefs about masculinity are only half as likely as men with more moderate masculine beliefs to get preventive healthcare.[182] Men have an aversion to therapy for the same reasons.[183] Men who adapt traditional notions of masculinity are more negative about seeking mental health services than those with more flexible gender attitudes.[184] While men report less depression than women, their depression is more lethal because they are less likely to seek help. Men complete suicide at far higher rates than women, and the numbers are moving in the wrong direction. The age-adjusted suicide rate for non-Hispanic white males increased twenty-eight percent between 1999 and 2014.[185]
- An attraction to dangerous risk-taking and delinquent behaviors. Research suggests that the more men conform to masculine norms, the more likely they are to

> normalize and engage in risky behaviors such as heavy drinking and using tobacco.[186]

These hypermasculine defenses are certainly not limited to any particular culture. In an odd twist, China has become increasingly concerned that their one-child policy has resulted in a generation of boys who are "too coddled and feminine" and that "video games, masturbation, and a lack of exercise (are) erasing the gender characteristics of a man who is not afraid of death and hardship." In response to these concerns, China has set up special schools in the United States to train their boys to be "real men." These schools promise to "never cultivate sissies," and that "when one of them cries, we will definitely not comfort him. We will only encourage him to be strong."[187]

In any culture, when these defenses are not sufficient to reassure men's insecure masculinity, they sometimes escalate the use of aggression and violence to reassure their precarious sense of their own masculinity.

Intimate Partner Violence

In general, people only feel the need to control and suppress what is most threatening to them. It follows then that men's controlling and abusive behavior towards women reflects their fear of women. Among dogs "True alphas rarely have to assert themselves within the pack, rarely have to act with aggression, bark orders, or use physical means of control . . .True alphas command authority . . . asserting their power only when necessary . . . If a so-called alpha needs to . . . yell, scream bully or attack . . . you have encountered an insecure alpha."[188]

Men's abusive behavior towards women has always been hidden in plain sight. Thirty-five percent of women worldwide experience physical and/or sexualized violence from a man in their lifetimes.[189] The United Nations recently identified the mistreatment of women and girls as one of the top three global problems hindering development.[190] As a culture, we are only now slowly and often grudgingly beginning to recognize this abuse, with the predictable and inevitable backlash from men defending their privilege that has followed.

The position of the American Psychological Association is that Intimate Partner Violence (IPV) is not a diagnosable mental illness, but part of a larger effort to control women as an element of the larger patriarchy.[191] A finer grain analysis reveals that IPV is not so much a result of men's desire to acquire or maintain power over women, but more about their fears of losing their power in relationships.[192] Men who endorse the values of hostile sexism—a prejudiced, often-aggressive antagonism towards women—are more vigilant about any signs of potential restriction of power in their intimate relationships. They are more likely to believe that they are at risk of losing power to a woman in an intimate relationship, which makes them more likely to resort to violence to restore or maintain that power .[193,194,195,196] Men who see themselves as being more disadvantaged in their intimate relationships with women are more often aggressive in those relationships.[197] In sum, the fear of loss of power was more predictive of aggression towards women than the desire for greater power.

The Political Impact of Men's Fears of Women

On a larger scale, men's femiphobia has an enormous impact on our political system. An argument can be made that politics is dominated by masculine anxiety. Essentially, people are successful in elections to the extent they are able present themselves as not feminine and are punished by the voters to the extent that they are perceived as feminine. For example, Bill Clinton was criticized when he was president for being dominated by his wife, but when his affair with Monica Lewinsky came out, his approval rating went up.[198]

In contrast, Hillary Clinton becoming the first national female presidential candidate of any of the major political parties in the United States sparked an unprecedented, misogynist backlash. Fifty-two percent of white men rated her as "highly unfavorable," the highest such rating for any Democratic nominee in over 35 years. We can reasonably conclude that these voter's antipathy towards Clinton was based on her gender by some of the signs displayed at the Republican convention: "Don't be a pussy. Vote for Trump." "Trump 2016: Finally someone with balls." "Hillary sucks but not like Monica." "Hillary special: 2 fat thighs, 2 small breasts, left wing."[199]

In our culture, the loud, angry endorsement of particular political views has been a time-honored way to demonstrate one's masculine credentials. Men who hold more conservative political views tended to adhere more rigidly to conventional gender role expectations and have a greater fear of femininity than males who hold more liberal political views.[200] For example, men who were given the suggestion that they were less masculine subsequently expressed more support for war and had more homophobic attitudes.[201]

Men who self-identify as liberal are more comfortable with political values that they associate as feminine, such as "the caregiving functions of the State . . . such as food stamps, aid for housing, and childcare as feminine values." Men who self-identify as conservative object to these political values not so much because of the financial cost, but more because they believe that programs like these create dependency, which is a stereotypically feminine value.[202] These men are also opposed to environmental protection legislation, seeing jobs as masculine, and the protection of Mother Earth as feminine.

Former President Trump is a national figure who regularly engages in displays of hypermasculinity, such as publicly bragging about the size of his penis[203] and his high levels of testosterone.[204] If toxic masculinity is a defense against fragile masculinity, it follows that men who are drawn to Mr. Trump's hypermasculine posturing would be men who feel less secure about their own masculinity. In fact, in the 2016 presidential election, Mr. Trump did better in districts in which men searched on the internet more often for terms such as "erectile dysfunction" and "how to get girls." Again, in the 2018 mid-term elections, support for Republican candidates was higher in districts in which Google search data suggested higher levels of fragile masculinity.

Men are confused. They're conflicted. They want a woman who's their intellectual equal, but they're afraid of women like that. They want a woman they can dominate, but then they hate her for being weak. It's an ambivalence that goes back to a man's relationship with his mother. Source of his life, center of his universe, object of both his fear and his love.

~~ Diane Frolove

CHAPTER THIRTEEN

UNDERLYING CAUSES OF MEN'S FEARS OF WOMEN

In this chapter, we examine evolutionary, sociocultural and psychological theories that can help us understand the origins of men's fears of women. Wanting to understand the cause of something is a natural inclination. However, focusing on the "why" can interfere with acknowledging the reality of a situation and facing whatever actions or personal transformations are required. This chapter's focus on the underlying causes of men's fears of women builds a bridge to the next section of the book on resolving those fears.

Evolutionary Factors

On an evolutionary level, most women reproduce, but only about two-thirds of men ever will, so there is an inherent competition among men for the scarce resource of a breeding partner.[205] This leads men to a focus on competition with other men at the expense of friendships, and to fear the loss of their hard-earned, easily lost, and difficult to replace breeding partner. After all, a male lion will kill the cubs of a lioness in order to sire his own cubs with her.[206]

"Just because you are paranoid doesn't mean they aren't after you."

~~ Joseph Heller, Catch 22

Sociocultural Factors

This is a challenging section of the book. It is difficult to write about the legitimate threats to the hegemony men have enjoyed for years without sounding like I am undermining legitimate feminist critiques of the patriarchy by equating men's fears with the far more dangerous fears that women live with every day. I do not want to be misunderstood and mistaken as an advocate for the paranoid and dangerous Men's Rights Movement.

When I studied the Rorschach inkblot test in graduate school, I learned that even the most paranoid delusional perceptions have at least some tenuous connection to reality. A paranoid patient will tell you what they see in a particular inkblot, and although you can't see it at first, if you ask them to show you where they saw it, and you get close enough to see the tiniest detail, you will see what they were basing their perception on. Of course, their interpretation of that detail is likely to be delusional and difficult to follow, but they are seeing that tiny piece of reality quite accurately. It would be easy to skip the subject of societal threats to men in order to avoid painful misinterpretations but doing so would be a profound disservice to the men I am working to understand, and to their female partners as well.

Despite overwhelming privilege and advantage in almost every area of their lives, men do actually have legitimate reasons to be scared about losing that advantage. The man on the top of the see-saw in the graphic in the Introduction of this book is not paranoid. He is accurately assessing the very real risk that the woman at the bottom will topple him from his perch by simply walking away. His privileged position is completely dependent on her remaining in her place.

Atlantic magazine ran a cover story in 2010 entitled, "The End of Men: How Women are Taking Control of Everything."[207] The author's premise was that technological and economic changes in the world have made men's physiologically-based domination obsolete and that the cognitive abilities and interpersonal skills more often developed by women are becoming more dominant. For most of recorded history, couples have shown a strong preference for male offspring. This is the first time in history that polling data suggests that couples have a preference for girls.

Women now dominate in most academic settings. Sixty-percent of graduates receiving a bachelor's or master's degree are women, as are half of those receiving law and medical degrees. Even forty-percent of those receiving an MBA, a traditionally male-dominated degree, are now women. It has gotten to the point that some of the elite private liberal arts colleges are applying affirmative action plans to male applicants.[208]

The same is true in the work force. Seventy-five percent of the jobs lost in the last recession were held by men. Of the fifteen job categories projected to grow the most in the next decade in the U.S., all but two are held primarily by women. Women now hold over fifty percent of managerial and professional jobs, which has almost doubled since 1980. This trend is likely to continue because research suggests that firms with women in upper management positions do better. The Organization of Economic Cooperative and Development measured the economic and political power of women in 162 countries in 2006 and found that the greater the power of women in a country, the greater the country's economic success.[209] Aid agencies recognize this phenomenon and are starting to make aid contingent on programs to empower and promote women.

These changes in the workplace have a powerful impact on families. In 1970, women contributed only 2.6 percent of the income in the average family. That number has increased almost twenty-fold to 42.2 percent. As women earn more and gain more financial independence, they are less dependent on men for financial support and marry less frequently. In 1970, eighty-four percent of women aged thirty to forty-four were married, but only sixty percent were in 2017.

The men who feel exploited and scared about these changes in the economic landscape are the ones who have spawned the new Men's Rights Movement, a loosely organized collection of misogynistic individuals and organizations, organized as a backlash against feminism, some of which the Southern Poverty Law Center has categorized as being part of a hate ideology under the umbrella of "male supremacy."

The bottom line is that things are not going well for white, uneducated men.[210] While mortality continues to fall among education classes in the developed world, middle-aged non-Hispanic white men with less than a high school diploma are one of the few groups experiencing an increase in mid-life mortality since the 1990s. These are "deaths of despair," thought to be primarily attributable to drug and alcohol use and to suicide.

Early Psychoanalytic Theories

Early writers in the field of psychology understood the importance of men's fears of women over one hundred years ago. Freud thought that some of the deepest parts of analysis were reached when men confronted their castration anxiety, the fear of emasculation by women in both the literal and symbolic sense, which he regarded as a universal experience in men.[211] As discussed in Chapter Two, this fear is represented in cultures around the world in symbols of vaginas with teeth. In adult men, this anxiety is expressed in men's extreme sensitivity to any perceived slights from women and the language men use whenever they feel threatened by women, calling them "castrating" or "ball busters."[212]

Freud accurately heard his patient's unconscious references to their primitive unconscious fears of being devoured by women, and he understood this as a reflection of the young men's conflict between the tender connection of his youth with his mother and their desire for the masculine power represented by their father.[213] Later analytic writers wrote about men's fears of being drawn in and destroyed by their longing for women, citing myths such as Ulysses and Samson as examples. For Horney, these fears are the cause of men's fragile sense of masculinity, and their use of hypermasculine defenses to defend their insecurity.[214]

Freud had a complicated relationship with women himself that suggests a good deal of his own fear. He elevated women to positions of influence within his organization, while simultaneously theorizing they were morally inferior because they did not have fully developed super egos.[215] Freud famously wrote, "The great question that has never been answered, and which I have not yet been able to answer, despite my thirty years of research into the feminine soul, is 'What does a woman want?"[216]

Attachment Theory

Another psychological theory that provides helpful perspective for understanding the roots of men's fears of women in intimate relationships is attachment theory.[217,218] Research suggests that the quality of a child's early emotional attachments sets the pattern for how that child responds to perceived hurts, separations, or threats of loss or abandonment in adult relationships.[219] There are three broad styles of early childhood attachment.

1. When a child's early caregivers were consistently available and adequately attended to their emotional needs, that child is likely to be securely attached to their primary caregiver, and to develop relationships with intimate partners as an adult in which they are also securely attached. Securely attached people are attracted to intimacy as an adult and are not easily threatened by conflict or temporary breaches of connection.
2. When a child's early caregivers were not consistently available and were unpredictable in the ways they attended to that child's needs, the child is likely to be anxiously attached to their primary caregiver and to develop relationships with intimate partners as an adult

in which they are also anxiously attached. People who are anxiously attached crave intimacy and closeness but worry a lot about conflict or anything else that suggests a potential break in connection.

3. When a child's early care givers were generally inattentive and did not do a very good job of attending to their needs, that child is likely to be avoidantly attached to their primary caregiver, and if they do develop relationships with intimate partners, they are likely to be avoidantly attached in those relationships. People who are avoidantly attached feel uncomfortable with too much closeness and may even see closeness as a threat.

Returning to our story about Tom and Lisa in Chapter Eleven, Tom looked a lot like someone who is avoidantly attached and Lisa looked like she is anxiously attached. Lisa being openly hurt and angry made Tom uncomfortable, so he did what avoidantly attached people do; he withdrew. Tom's withdrawal triggered Lisa's fears of being abandoned and she did what anxiously attached people often do; she pursued. Remember in the TAT study mentioned earlier that the intimacy that women wanted most in relationships is what was most threatening to men.

In fact, noted couples' researcher John Gottman found that seventy percent of the difficulties in heterosexual relationships are attributable to men who are avoidantly attached being partnered with women who are anxiously attached.[220] If that is correct, then perhaps men's fears of women are not as universal as I've suggested. Maybe men are only afraid of women when avoidantly attached men partner with anxiously attached women.

I don't doubt that men who are insecurely attached have greater fears of women than men who are more securely attached. However, men's fears of women are certainly not limited to men who are insecurely attached. It is true that men who are avoidantly attached have higher Gender Role Conflict than men with other attachment styles.[221] However, the majority of men in a non-clinical sample are securely attached, and there is little evidence of gender difference in attachment styles, and what exists is largely learned as it is essentially non-existent in children.[222] Given the prevalence of men's fears of women, if those fears were attributable to an avoidant attachment style then there would have to be a preponderance of men with an avoidant attachment style, which is not the case.

There is another explanation that I think is a better fit for the data. Gottman correctly observed that in the majority of couples conflict, men appear to be avoidantly attached and women appear to be anxiously attached. However, Gottman interpreted this observation through an exclusively psychological lens, specifically through the lens of attachment theory. When seen through a larger sociocultural lens, the patriarchal culture as a whole shapes men to be more avoidant and women to be more anxious. The patriarchy creates Gender Role Conflict for men and puts them in an emotionally constricted position that makes it difficult for men to experience much intimacy in their relationships. This leads inevitably to a fear of women, because if you are impaired in your capacity to feel intimately connected with someone, you will naturally be more afraid of losing the connection.

Relational theory suggests that many of the traits that we consider to be characteristic of individual personality, i.e., that person is selfish, or that person is angry, and so forth, are more fully understood in their interpersonal context.[223] For example, the person we might judge as selfish might be behaving that way in response to a self-involved partner who never gives a thought to her welfare. The person we judge to be angry might be behaving that way in response to being gaslighted in a subtly abusive manner by her partner. Most therapists know that it is quite common to find men with narcissistic features partnered with women who have features of Borderline Personality Disorder. Seen through the lens of relational theory, we can see that any women married to a man with narcissistic tendencies is likely to look increasingly Borderline, just as any man married to a woman with features of Borderline Personality is going to look more Narcissistic.[224]

From this perspective, most of the conflict in heterosexual relationships involves men who are behaving avoidantly and women who are behaving anxiously because, regardless of their overall attachment style, men tend to resort to avoidant defenses when threatened by the intimacy of a relationship, just as women tend to resort to anxious defenses in response to their partners' withdrawal. Men look less avoidant when they are not partnered with someone who has been polarized into an anxious position, and women look less anxious when they are not partnered with someone who has been polarized into an avoidant role. Men are socialized to fear intimacy as feminine and adapt an avoidant defense as masculine. Women are socialized to desire intimacy and to adopt an anxious defense when they don't get it, having learned from their mothers that it is probably the only way they can elicit any kind of connection from their partners, no matter how unsatisfying that stilted connection is.

Tom withdraws when Lisa gets more emotional because he is uncomfortable with her open expression of emotions, so he modulates his discomfort with his preferred strategy of withdrawal. Tom's preference for withdrawal as his first line of defense is not so much an expression of a particular attachment style, because most men detach in the face of pressures for intimacy regardless of their attachment style. Tom's withdrawal confirms Lisa's worst fears of being abandoned and escalates her level of emotional distress. The conflict escalates because what Lisa needs the most terrifies Tom.

Fatherless Children

> *In intimate relations between a man and a woman, he is in one very important respect more vulnerable than she is: She can readily re-evoke in him the unqualified, boundless helpless passion of infancy. If he lets her, she can shatter his adult sense of power and control; she can bring out the soft, wild, naked baby in him.*[225]
>
> ~~ Dorothy Dinnerstein

The patriarchy powerfully shapes intimate relationships by socializing men and women into certain narrowly constrained gender roles, as covered in Chapter Eleven. As far back as we know, women (either mothers or paid helpers) have had the primary responsibility for rearing children. Women are socialized from an early age to learn how to be the primary caregiver for children and to spend their childhoods rehearsing for that role. Men are socialized to think of their work as being outside of the family (or at least outside of the home, i.e., taking care of the yard) and to think of themselves as both less capable and less responsible for the care of children. Having been socialized from an early age to develop their competitive and aggressive skills, boys do not have nearly the practice or opportunity to develop the skills in relationships or childrearing that their female partners have. Boys typically do not grow up playing house or with baby dolls, and often get very little experience caring for any younger siblings.

My ex-wife had a Cesarean section with our first child and was confined to bed for the first three weeks, meaning that outside of nursing, I was in charge of pretty much everything having to do with the care of the child and the house. The house part I could manage pretty well. I had lived on my own and had some idea of what was needed. The childcare part, on the other hand, both terrified and puzzled me. I remember how scared I was the first time I held our son. I had no idea how to do it, because even though I have two younger sisters, I don't think I had ever held a baby in my life. I have a picture of me giving my son his first bath, holding the baby in one hand and the notes from the child birthing class in the other. I had no idea how to bathe a baby, but I was a graduate student, and I knew how to take notes and follow directions.

In the womb, infants experience perfect care and nurturing. All their needs are seamlessly met before they can even recognize that such a thing as a need exists. No words are needed. Infants cry when they are born because they are expelled from the garden. They are cold, exposed, the first light they see is blinding, and they have no words and can only wail in protest. An infant's first post-birth attachment is typically to the mother, so the earliest experience of pleasure is with her—preverbal, and primarily through physical contact. Infants are held and soothed by women and feel safe in a woman's arms. Emotional experiences that happen during the preverbal period are the most enduring because they are less readily influenced by verbal, rational processes later in life. It is not until adulthood, through an erotic connection with another person that we ever rediscover some of the intensity of those early feelings. In some ways, men yearn for the perfect love they experienced as a child with a woman for the rest of their lives, and they resent the women in their adults lives for not giving that to them.

Childrearing being the exclusive domain of women initially followed naturally from biology, but technological advances have made this polarization almost completely unnecessary. Yet the polarization persists, despite being largely unsatisfying to both men and women and to the detriment of their children, and the cause of much tension and conflict in heterosexual relationships.[226]

Women have been trying to tell us for centuries how this arrangement constrains their lives, but we are also starting to look at how it limits the lives of men. Women assuming the role as primary, or sole, caregiver has led them to develop competencies related to empathic attunement and care, and an increased awareness of and responsibility for relationships and social networks. At the same time, women have fewer opportunities to develop their capacities for independence and individuation, to pursue their own interests with less regard for the impact on others, which costs them dearly in workplaces that highly value those qualities. Men, of course, have lots of opportunities to develop those qualities that serve them well in the workplace, but typically far fewer opportunities to develop the competencies they need to thrive in intimate relationships and families. I always recommend to new fathers that they be the ones to get up in the middle of the night with their new infants. They often protest that they should be the ones to sleep at night because they work in the mornings, and I suggest that the unsupervised intimacy they can have with their children in the middle of the night is far more important than missed sleep.

In infancy, women are most often the source of an infant's first experiences of bliss and merger that rival the perfection experienced in the womb. Mom can take away the pain with just one kiss, or calm the terror with a single warm embrace, or bring elusive sleep by cuddling and singing. Infants depend on this secure feeling of attachment to their caregivers as much as they depend on them for food and safety. They quickly learn which behaviors most consistently elicit the kind of nurturing they cannot live without—smiling, making cute noises, reaching out. A mutual conversation ensues between infant and caregiver, each learning the behaviors that most consistently elicit attachment behaviors from each other.[227]

Then there is the inevitable fall from the garden. Try as they might, no caregiver can provide the kind of perfect seamless care that the infant experienced in the womb. Inevitably there are gaps, moments when a child's needs are not adequately met, or when the gratification of those needs is delayed without warning or explanation. There are dysregulating moments when their mother is distracted or otherwise unavailable, when her touch does not magically soothe the pain or distress, or she is non-responsive to the terror, or impatient or even angry with an infant's struggles to sleep.

Children who grow up in families with only one emotionally engaged caretaker are likely to experience more of these gaps than those raised in families with two or more emotionally engaged caregivers. Ideally, the inevitable gaps in caregiving that every child experiences are infrequent and insignificant enough that they actually help the child develop emotional resilience and the capacity for self-soothing. However, when the primary caregiver is unable to provide emotional caregiving on a reasonably consistent basis, when the gaps in caring are more than the child can overcome, that child is likely to develop an attachment to his caregiver that is anxious or insecure.

Anyone who has cared for a baby knows the panicked feeling of trying to soothe a wailing child, desperately trying everything they can think of to soothe the child as well as themselves. Is he hungry? Wet? Tired? Remember in the Still Face experiments how quickly the children became dysregulated in response to caretaker behavior that was not abusive, but just the withdrawal of attention and affirmation from their caregiver.[228]

> *For the infant, the mother who had previously been the source of perfect union and bliss now also becomes the source of pain, frustration, and disappointment. Mother now also becomes the first adversary, the first experience of needing something from someone who only sometimes provides it, sometimes neglects to provide it, and sometimes withholds it. It is a contest the infant cannot hope to win because their mother has jurisdiction over the child's body, through her control over what goes into it and what comes out of it, through*

her right to restrict its movements and invade its orifices, to withhold pleasure or inflict pain until it obeys her wishes. Each human being first discovers the peculiarly angry, bittersweet experience of conscious surrender to conscious, determined outside rule.[229]

Infants respond by desperately trying to figure out which behaviors sustain and repair the needed attachment, and which behaviors put it at risk. Infants also have their first experiences of subordinating their own desires in the interest of being cared for and loved by their female care givers. Nothing is more important than doing what pleases her, and they devote themselves to anticipating her wishes and making them their own.

As boys get older and more interested in their fathers and the world of men, their fathers then get more comfortable with having a relationship with their sons, as long as it is on Dad's terms and doesn't present too much of a challenge to him. This often happens around sports, which is an arena that is comfortable to many dads, and a way to entice a son to become interested in the masculine world of competition and aggression. This is the quintessential example of a father coaching his son's team, driving the process with his own interests and desire to relive his own frustrated athletic dreams (I could a' been a contender!), or a father dragging his son along with him on the golf course, beaming in the narcissistic glow of having his son with him and not noticing that the child is bored out of his mind but afraid to let his dad know he is not having a good time.

Boys' fathers are generally more remote, less available, and less engaged than their moms, but dads clearly represent the power and privilege of the world outside of the family. They operate effectively in that outside world and bring those resources back home to support the family. The clear message to boys is that their attachment to the closeness they have shared with their mothers is seen as an obstacle to their obtaining this newfound status as a man, i.e., there are only two choices, you can be a man or you can be a mamma's boy. This is an internal dilemma for boys, as their mothers remain the reference point for everything. Jumping off the diving board is no fun unless mom is watching. All masculine striving to be effective in the world, as well as competition with other men, is done with an eye towards mother and her approval.

There is a seemingly irreconcilable conflict between wanting to hold onto the nurturance boys experience primarily if not exclusively with their mothers while also joining the world of power and privilege offered by their fathers. Boys gradually become aware that lingering identification with their mothers is an obstacle to joining this new world. The resolution for many men is to keep their emotional attachment and dependency on women well hidden, from others and from themselves, and to secure their place in the world of men by proving that they do not really need women, and even on some level disdain them. Restricting their level of attachment to women is one of the primary methods men use to help control their fears of women. Men do this by some combination of not letting themselves know what they feel, not letting themselves feel too much, and not letting their partner know how they feel.

Men are required to be more emotionally constricted and more separated from their own interior lives. This impoverishes them emotionally and even limits the intensity of physical pleasure they can allow themselves. Men cope by restricting their capacity to feel and to be intimate with others. In this sense, men are more damaged than women by this arrangement.[230]

When men talk about the agony of being men, they can never quite get away from the recurrent theme of self-pity. And when women talk about being women, they can never quite get away from the recurrent theme of blaming men.

~~ Pat Conroy, The Prince of Tides

SECTION IV

RESOLVING MEN'S FEARS

This last section of the book is about how to resolve the fears discussed up to this point. The three chapters that follow offer resolutions to the problems men's fears cause themselves, their partners, their relationships, and society-at-large. In these chapters, I address men helping themselves, men helping other men, and men and women helping each other.

You, the reader, will no doubt detect a shift in tone from the prior parts of this book. Up until now, my aim has been to present theoretical perspectives, research findings, and clinical observations about men's fears of women. While my intent has been to present that information in a relatable, accessible way, the tone has been unapologetically academic. This last section speaks directly to you and how you as a man, or as a woman reading this to better understand your partner, or as a couple, can work on these issues and find greater peace, satisfaction, and fulfillment in your relationships.

The only men who aren't in fear of women's reactions are usually men who aren't born or who are dead.

~~ Warren Farrell

Chapter Fourteen

Men Helping Themselves

If you've read this far, you have a pretty good idea of what men's fears of women look like in intimate relationships and the culture at large, some sense of how those fears might play out in your own life or your relationships, and some ideas about what causes those fears. Here, we take up the question of what to do about those fears.

The reflexive answer to that question is often, "Get rid of them!" I don't blame you. Fear is unpleasant, and most of us do what we can to avoid situations that frighten us. Tempting as it may be to avoid or deny things that scare us, we talked earlier about how fear can be adaptive when it alerts us to real danger. There is an optimum level of fear in any situation, a level of fear that is proportional to the level of threat and proportional to the circumstances. Having more fear than the situation calls for is obviously not ideal, but so is having less fear than the situation calls for.

For example, if someone you are in a relationship with recently hurt you badly and has so far shown no remorse, it is probably smart to be at least a little cautious about how much you want to risk in that relationship moving forward. It would be a bit reckless to make yourself even more vulnerable before you are clear whether you have a reliable partner in that venture. On the other hand, fears can become exaggerated to the extent that they are counter-productive and constrain our lives unnecessarily. If you approach the conversation with your partner so guarded against further hurt that you are unable to hear her or open your heart in response to your partner's genuine expression of remorse and regard for you, things are not likely to go well.

The problem is, as you will read later in this chapter, trying to eliminate fear will most likely make you more scared, just as trying to suppress any emotion most often increases the intensity of that emotion. In general, more harm comes from all the defenses used to guard against our fears than the experience of fear itself.

Rather than working to avoid your fears of women, allow me to suggest that you consider aiming for the resolution of your fears. To resolve a fear means "[to] deal with successfully, find an answer, to make clear or understandable."[231]

Recognizing When You Might Be Scared

Simply recognizing that you are scared is by itself a powerful first step towards resolving that fear. Awareness alone is not enough to bring about change, but becoming aware of your fears of women is very likely to set the process of change in motion.[232]

My first step in working with men is to look for opportunities to use the words "scared" or "afraid" in our conversations. These words can be used in reference to anything, large or small. It's like the Zen Koan, "What is the sound of one hand clapping." It's meant to get men thinking, considering the idea that they might in fact be scared. Men generally respond in similar ways, first reflexively denying that they are scared because that's what they have been taught to do, to deny to themselves, and anyone else that they are afraid of anything, much less a woman. It's noteworthy how little time goes by before you see a puzzled look on their faces as they begin to consider that what they are feeling might be fear, followed remarkably quickly by the realization just how often they have been afraid of the important women in their lives. For many men, this new realization changes a lot of how they think about themselves and their intimate relationships.

If you are a man reading this, you may have had a similar experience with this book, rejecting it at first because it didn't remotely seem possible to you. But if you've read this far, you have probably recognized yourself somewhere along the way. I suggest you try carrying around the idea that you are afraid of women like a filter, a standing question that you pose to yourself any time you think it might be relevant. Ask yourself:

- Is it possible that what I'm feeling in this interaction with my partner is fear?
- It seems to be that I am mostly angry, but might there be fear underneath that anger?
- If I am afraid, how would that change my understanding of what is going on with me?
- How would my understanding of what is going on between us change if I try it on with that filter?

Here are some situations in which men are often afraid of women. Consider trying out your filter if you find yourself in any of these.

- Any interaction with a woman who is assertive or in a hierarchically superior position to you;
- Any perceived loss of some part of traditional male status or power, such as unemployment, physical limitations, etc;
- Any situation in which you feel vulnerable with a woman, particularly if you believe that vulnerability will be a weakness or a liability;
- Any intimate situation with a woman, particularly if you perceive the woman as pushing for greater intimacy;
- Any loss in a competitive situation with other men, or any situation in which you have homoerotic feelings.

I particularly encourage you to considering the possibility that you are scared of women any time you find yourself defensive or angry, particularly when the level of your defensiveness or anger seems out of proportion to what's going on. That kind of disproportionate reaction often suggests underlying fear.

Men are, of course, are quite capable of the full range of emotional experience, but there are a lot of social prohibitions against men expressing any emotion other than anger. Fear is a vulnerable emotion and men are taught to hide any vulnerability as a sign of weakness that is feminine and puts you at a competitive disadvantage with other men. Any sign of fear in the aggressive hyper-competitive world of men is most often met with derision or taunts from other men about being feminine. It is most masculine either to not acknowledge feeling afraid in situations that are obviously dangerous, or to acknowledge fear only to highlight your bravery in overcoming the fear by acting heroically. Anger appeals to men because they can be angry and still remain well defended and not vulnerable. Anger helps men feel more in control of their own emotional experience, and it can also be used as a weapon to intimidate and control women when men feel threatened.

Consider some of these everyday situations in which anger might be masking your underlying fear.

- You're angry that your partner spends so much time texting and talking on the phone with her friends. Might this be masking your fears that she does not enjoy talking with you as much as she does with her friends?
- You're angry at your partner for coming home late from work and bringing work home with her. Might your anger be masking your fears about her being more successful than you?
- You're angry at always being criticized by your partner, to the point that you can't ever seem to get it right. Is this masking your fears of not being able to please her?
- You're angry that the kids always come first with your partner and she never seems to have any time for you. Is anger masking your fear that you don't really know

how to have the kind of close relationship that she has with the kids?

"We cannot change, we cannot move away from what we are, until we thoroughly accept what we are. Then changes seems to come about almost unnoticed."

~~ Carl Rogers

Embracing the Fear

Given the significant prohibitions against men feeling fear, it may seem odd or even somewhat threatening for me to suggest that the best way for you to resolve your fears of women in intimate relationships is to fully embrace those fears. I do understand that every instinct tells you to push away your fears of women and to act like you are not scared even if you know you are. The problem is that whenever you disown any aspect of your experience, all you are doing is killing the messenger. The message itself just goes underground, only to emerge later, stronger than ever. As in most things, the more actively any need is suppressed, the more frequent and stronger the need becomes. Try skipping lunch today and then try to talk yourself into not being hungry, and see if you don't feel hungrier.

The denial of men's fears is the cause of much of their emotional suffering. These suppressed emotions don't just magically go away. Their remnants linger, and men tend to either internalize those fears as depression and/or low self-esteem or even self-loathing, or they turn those unacknowledged fears outwards in the form of anger and aggression.[233]

Ronaldo had a terribly painful breakup. He was convinced that Darla was the one for him, and they were actively making plans for a life together when Darla broke up with him without explanation. Wanting to avoid reexperiencing something that painful in the future, but not wanting to be alone, Ronaldo came up with the ingenious solution of continuing to date but never allowing himself to get very emotionally involved with anyone. It is not something he consciously planned, it's just what happened.

Ronaldo unconsciously found a solution that makes it unlikely that he will have his heart broken in the same way again. However, this solution requires Ronaldo to ignore his deep-seated desires to trust again in order to have the kind of emotional openness and connection with a woman that pushed him to take those risks with Darla in the first place.

What Ronaldo most needs to recover from his traumatic breakup with Darla and be more available for an intimate relationship with another woman is a redo rather than an avoidance. If you are bitten by a dog as a child, you may develop a phobia of dogs to protect yourself from being retraumatized in that particular way. The problem is that every time you avoid contact with a dog, you are reinforcing your trauma-induced belief that dogs are dangerous. The treatment for a dog phobia is to gradually approach dogs, taking it very slowly, one step at time, always stopping when you get too scared, until gradually you learn that not all dogs are dangerous. The only way for Ronaldo to resolve his fear of being abandoned is to gradually allow himself to risk more closeness with a woman, having the courage to check in with himself and with her along the way to see how things are going, and then make adjustments to his level of risk and vulnerability in the relationship based on how that goes. Change happens through experience.

Paradoxically, the surest way to exaggerate anything you feel is to work hard to stop yourself from feeling it. For example, men's concerns about erectile dysfunction is a major contributor to erectile dysfunction in men. The best way to bring your fear in line with the circumstances is to embrace that fear rather than trying to block it. Embracing fear is the best way to change it because our lives are like a river, dynamic and always flowing. The river of our experience can move swiftly or meander slowly, sometimes take a straight path, and other times twist in unexpected directions. The water can be smooth and calm or turbulent and rocky, but it is always moving.

Embracing fear is like swimming in the river of life, what the Buddhists call "being in the flow." The more you are able to embrace your fear, to immerse yourself fully in the flow of your fear, the faster the fear will line up with the circumstances. The more you distance from your fear, the longer you will stay stuck.

The process of embracing your fear can seem counter-intuitive at first. Our first instinct is often to pull away from the very experiences we need to change. Embracing your fear simply means allowing yourself to feel whatever you feel, with as few preconceptions about what it should feel like, and as little judgment as possible. Embracing your fear means being as fully present to the feeling as you can, engaging and moving further into your experience of fear rather than pulling away or distracting yourself. It means paying attention to anything that you notice along with the fear—your thoughts, other feelings, fantasies, memories, bodily sensations, and intuition. Any kind of experience you have is wisdom from deeper inside of you. Pay attention to it.

In order to embrace your fear, you'll have to learn how to let go of all the clever distractions you've developed over the years to distract yourself from the fear, sometimes known as ways of "acting out," meaning any action taken to avoid feeling. Drugs and alcohol are popular forms of acting out. Extramarital affairs are another common way of acting out rather than feeling whatever is going on in the relationship. Over-functioning and co-dependency are also very common ways of acting out, especially for women, rather than facing their fears of inadequacy or abandonment. Most of our life's struggles are the result of acting out rather than embracing our feelings.

Take a moment, close your eyes, and think about something that frightens you. It doesn't matter what it is. Let yourself imagine it until you can actually *feel* scared. What do you notice? If you are like most people, you will notice tightness someplace in your body. It might be in your chest, or your neck. It's different for different people, but most people contract their muscles when they feel fear. The same thing happens emotionally. When we are scared, we tighten, we constrict, become less emotionally open, less vulnerable. The problem is that being vulnerable and emotionally open are required in order to get emotionally close to someone. In other words, fear interferes with our capacity to be intimate. Now imagine telling someone you love about the fear you are feeling. Imagine a look of compassionate acceptance on their face, perhaps they touch you or even hug you as you talk. See yourself relaxing into their embrace and letting yourself feel the fear more fully, letting go of the ways in which you have been holding back. As you go through this, pay attention to your level of fear, see if it doesn't relax significantly.

Psychotherapy

If you are feeling stuck in your efforts to resolve your fears of women in your intimate relationships, I recommend that you consider consulting a well-trained psychotherapist. A good therapist should help you learn how to embrace the full range of your experience, including your fears of women, and help guide you towards resolution.

Men often do not seek psychotherapy because they are socialized to believe that asking for help of any kind, but particularly psychological help, runs contrary to the masculine norm of self-reliance and is shameful, a sign of weakness.[234] Men are said to be reluctant even to ask for directions when they're lost. Men with higher Gender Role Conflict are less likely to seek help than those with less GRC, which means that men who have the strongest fears of women and need the most help are the least likely to seek it out.[235]

Therapy can be threatening to men because the therapist is most likely to be a woman,[236] but even if the therapist is a man, men anticipate being judged in therapy for being guarded or defensive, emotionally withdrawn, or not sufficiently vulnerable and emotionally open, recapitulating the same fears of inadequacy and not being able to "get it right" that they so painfully experience in their primary relationship. In couples' therapy, men worry that the therapist will be allied with their partner and that they will end up as the identified patient, the one who needs fixing.

You can work with either a male or female therapist—that's a matter of personal preference. I do recommend that you find a therapist who does a lot of work with men and has an understanding of men's fears of women in intimate relationships as described in this book or is willing to learn. Being male doesn't mean a therapist necessarily understands this, just as therapists who have had a drinking problem don't necessarily understand recovery.

It is truly unfortunate that we have created a situation in which men are reluctant to seek help from psychotherapy because there is a lot for men to gain, some of which is very different from what they might believe. Here is an abbreviated list of some of what men stand to gain in therapy. If some of these things are already true for you, congratulations. You've probably already done some good work in your life, whether in therapy or not, and deserve all that you have earned. I'll start with the ones that are more obvious, the ones you may already associate with therapy, and then move to some that may be more surprising to you.

You are likely to feel significantly less anxious and/or depressed. This is not surprising; most people expect this from a course of psychotherapy. The research is quite clear that psychotherapy is a very effective treatment for both anxiety and depression, and that it is dose dependent, meaning that the longer you stay the more help you are likely to receive.

You are likely to feel significantly less lonely. Men's power and privilege comes at the high cost of neglecting relationships and closeness, leaving many men profoundly isolated.[237] You have successfully kept yourself busy enough, along with your partner's seamless enabling, but try this experiment. Imagine your partner leaving town for the weekend and see what comes up for you. Do you feel uncomfortable, worried about how you will fill the time, or do you look forward to it as an opportunity to catch up with people you feel close to?

One that may surprise you is that even if you start individual therapy for yourself, you're still going to end up feeling much closer to your partner. It is likely that she will be less disappointed and angry with you, more interested in listening to you talk about your life, more emotionally supportive, more affectionate, and more interested in sex, which will be more satisfying for both of you.

If you have children, you will also probably feel much closer and more connected with them, more comfortable and even enthusiastic about being an active father. Again, imagine your partner tells you that she is going out of town for the weekend. Do you feel anxious, and start thinking about who you can get to help you with the kids, or do you look forward to the chance to spend more time with them?

Last, and perhaps least expected, people in therapy generally are more successful in their work, however they define that. This one is hard to explain, but it probably has to do with being able to be more fully yourself in the world.

Fathering

Noted feminist author Dinnerstein made the radical claim that we will never undo the patriarchy until men are fully involved in raising their children.[238] It is a radical thing to do. Potentially world changing. When my children were young, after changing I don't know how many diapers on the filthy sink counters of restaurants, I cried the first time I saw a changing station in a McDonald's men's room.

As mentioned earlier, I urge you to be the one to get up in the middle of the night with your kids. It's the only unsupervised time you'll get, and you can find your own way of being a dad without worrying about someone watching you. You will never regret it. Encourage your partner to take some time off, get away. Don't do it as a favor to her, tell her you want her to leave so that you can get some solid, uninterrupted time with the children. You'll figure it out.

One of the best ways for you as a man to heal whatever childhood wounds you have from the less-than-optimal parenting you may have received is to be the parent you wish you had. This is a mysterious process that I can't fully explain even though I have experienced it myself and witnessed it with many people in my office. When you have been wounded yourself, the first instinct is to feel shortchanged and look for payback. Paradoxically, giving someone else what you were deprived of constitutes an important part of the healing. For men, modeling a different kind of masculinity for their sons is often a crucial part of resolving their own gender role conflict and fear of women.

"There is no 'I' without a 'Thou'."

~~ Martin Buber

CHAPTER FIFTEEN

MEN HELPING EACH OTHER

While it might seem that each of us knows ourselves best, and that the optimal path to self-knowledge is introspection, the paradoxical truth is that we can only know ourselves fully through relationship. My over-simplified example to skeptical students is the case of our own rear ends. I have a pretty good idea what most of me looks like, although even there I am limited to the reverse image I can see in a mirror. At the same time, I know very little about what my rear end looks like. Try as I might to strain and turn around to see, even with a mirror I can only catch fleeting glimpses of what my *tush* looks like, and even then, I am seeing a twisted, distorted view. My wife, however, has a pretty good idea of what my rear end looks like.

We can only know ourselves fully through relationships because we can only <u>be</u> fully ourselves through in-depth engagement in intimate relationships. Each relationship, every intimate encounter with another person has the potential to evoke a different aspect of our potential self. This interpersonal theory has been scientifically validated by research in the field of epigenetics, which demonstrates that different aspects of our genetic potential are either actuated or inhibited by environmental experiences.[239] It's not just that we act and feel differently in the context of different relationships, it is that we literally are different people in each relationship. When a child is born, if someone picks that child up and gazes at him adoringly and holds him closely, that child understands himself as lovable in that moment and quite literally becomes lovable. He has no other frame of reference, he could not at that moment be anything else. If, however, that same child when born is cast aside in a trash bin, he not only will experience himself as unlovable but will literally be unlovable. Again, he could not at that moment be anything else. This helps explains the delicious excitement of falling in love, which can happen when we let down our guard enough to make room for the exciting new possibilities of who we might become.

After you've gone as far as you can in embracing your own fears of women, you need to start engaging in intimate conversations with other men in order to continue the work towards understanding and resolving those fears. While it is clear that those conversations eventually need to be with women, it is critically important you start with conversations with other men. There are a number of advantages to talking to other men before you start to talk with your partner.

First, although men are strongly socialized not to talk about anything personal with other men, especially not to reveal any fears that might lower their status in other men's eyes and create a competitive disadvantage, it is still easier to talk to other men than it is to talk to an intimate partner. Second, talking to other men will likely be the start of an exchange in which those other men will reciprocate by opening up about their experience with you. This dialogue will inevitably help you understand your own experience more fully. Lastly, if you have children, talking to other men is the kind of example you might want to set for your children. Whether you have a son or daughter, it is good to show them a different model of how men handle things than the model that you learned.

When psychotherapists get together to talk about their work, one of the things they often discuss is how difficult it is to work with men. Men tend to avoid therapy to begin with, and when they do come to therapy, their presence is often not completely voluntary. They have often been coerced or even threatened by their partners to go to individual therapy or to join them in couples' therapy. Most therapists have had a couple call for help, and then had the woman leave treatment very quickly, making it clear that she only came to get her partner into treatment because she was convinced he would never do it otherwise.

Men simply don't have much experience thinking about, much less talking about their own internal lives, so the experience of coming to therapy and being asked in an open-ended way to talk about what's going on with them feels like a request to speak in a language they do not understand. Therapists are accustomed to patients coming to them who are in a good deal of distress and have little difficulty talking about what is troubling with them. Therapists talk about working with men being like "pulling teeth," complaining that they have to put in a lot more of the energy, pursuing men to try to coerce them to talk about themselves.

I've been leading psychotherapy groups for fifty years, and because I work with a lot of men, I decided to start a group just for men. I was uncharacteristically anxious before the first meeting of this group. I thought I had made a huge mistake putting together a group of all men. It is most often the women in a mixed-gender therapy group who take the lead in being more emotionally open. The men often learn from the women and open up more over time. I anticipated that it would be very difficult getting the men in the room to talk to each other in any kind of meaningful personal way in a men's group.

I couldn't have been more wrong. I have never seen a group open up and share as quickly as that group did. The men were openly expressing feelings within the first hour, some of them crying openly, and the entire group decided to hug each other at the end of the group, something they still do every week, and none of my other groups do. What I learned is that the stereotype about men being reluctant to open up in therapy is mistaken. Men are actually dying to talk about their internal experience. Apparently, it's opening up to women that's more challenging.

To help you with this next step, I suggest that you consider forming a group with other men to work on these issues together. Start with people you know, men you think are interested in learning more about themselves and learning how to feel closer with other men. I would suggest starting with six to ten people. The more diverse the members are in terms of race, age, socioeconomic circumstances, and life experience, the richer the experience will be for everyone. I suggest you meet not less than once a month, more often if you like.

Ask everyone to read this book before the first meeting and use the book as a way to kick off your work together. From there, meetings should be open ended, with the group talking about whatever the members want to talk about that day. You can either function as a leaderless group or use a system of rotating leaders with a different member facilitating each meeting.

Here are some guidelines I suggest you consider adopting for your group.

1. First and foremost is confidentiality. Each member is asked to commit to not revealing anything said by anyone else in the group, or the identity of members of the group. Without this, you got nothing.

2. The group is a place to talk about your own experience. Talk about yourself and your experience. Don't tell other people about themselves or try to fix them or tell them what to do. Try to avoid giving advice.

3. Take your fair share of the time and do your fair share of the work. This means that each member commits to not taking more than their share of the time, but also to contributing enough to do their share of the work. Doing the work means talking about yourself in order to gain a better understanding of your fears of women and move towards resolution of those fears in order to be happier, closer to your partner and kids.

4. Take responsibility for everything you say and for what you don't say because they have equal impact on the group. Take responsibility for the way your words land on other people. Be interested in the impact of your words rather than defensive, even if you feel misunderstood or the impact was different from what you intended.

I've set up group on Facebook, "Understading Men's Fears of Women," where men who are interested in forming groups like this can talk with each other about their groups. Please visit and take a look at what other men are saying about their experiences in forming groups like this, and add something about your own experience or questions you have. I will monitor the group and am available for questions. This link is case sensitive:

https://bit.ly/MensFearsOfWomenAvrumWeissFBGroup

Notes

Men fear that becoming 'we' will erase his 'I.' For women, our 'we' is our saving grace.

~~ Jane Fonda

After sex, men fear too much intimacy; they want to separate again. Women want to talk, to continue the merging, melting fusion into one. Postcoital conversations keep the woman's power alive. Through unconscious severance, by falling asleep, the man regains his self.

~~ Nancy Friday

Chapter Sixteen

Couples Helping Each Other

In my psychotherapy practice, I first came to understand how scared men are of their partners. Time after time I listened to men recount the things they were unhappy about in their marriages—some insignificant, some every day, and some that seemed challenging enough to call the relationship into question. Each time, I asked these men "have you talked to your partner about any of this?" Almost immediately a horrified look came over their face as they explained to me that they were absolutely convinced that talking to their wives about what was bothering them would almost inevitably make it much worse and get them in more "trouble" than they were already in.

These men are not entirely wrong. Talking to your partner about your fears may lead to additional conflict in the relationship, at least initially. At the same time, talking with your partner is the only way to fully resolve these fears. Keep in mind that your partner wants this to go well just as much as you do. She may lose track of that at times, just as you do, but you can gently remind each other that you are both on the same side. Talking to your partner about your fears is taking a risk, but it also opens the door to living a healthier life, one in which you can be less scared to be more fully yourself, and able to feel much closer to the people you love and who love you.

Stereotypically, couples often think that the frequency of conflict is one of the best indicators of how things are going. People in a new relationship often say that things are going really well because "we never argue." However, research makes it clear that the frequency of conflict is not an indication of trouble in a relationship. In fact, research indicates that couples feel relieved, happier, and more optimistic about the future of the relationship when they take the risk of talking to their partner about their dissatisfactions in the relationship. On the other hand, the way a couple argues does have a lot to do with how well things go.[240] According to the Gottman Institute, highly respected researchers in the field of couple's relationships, there are four communication styles, or psychological defenses, that often predict the end of a relationship.[241]

- Criticism. Being critical of who the other person is, rather than talking about how your partner's behavior impacts you.
- Contempt. This is where criticism escalates, when one partner disrespects the other and is derisive, contemptuous, and sometimes intentionally hurtful towards the other. Contempt is the single strongest predictor of divorce.
- Defensiveness. This can be a response to real or imagined criticism when people are feeling particularly insecure in their relationships.

- Stonewalling. This can be a response to real or imagined contempt when people are feeling particularly insecure in their relationship.

Ideally both partners in a relationship would work towards using all four of these defense mechanisms less often. However, women are more likely to utilize the first two of these defenses—criticism and contempt—and are best served by focusing on them. Men tend to adopt the second two of the defenses—defensiveness and stonewalling—and would do best to focus on those.

Let's start by reviewing some of the material from Chapter Eleven on the impact of men's fears of women on couples. When couples first come together, there is often a period of intense, mutual interdependency. Each person's life is changed, often dramatically for the better, and neither wants to take any risks that might mess things up. In this delightful honeymoon period, couples tend to accentuate all of the positives in their new relationship and avoid paying too much attention to anything else. Any kind of separation can feel threatening, whether it is physical separation or the kind of separation that happens as you gradually recognize that you and your new partner have differences.

Over time, as couples begin to feel more secure with each other, the intensity of this mutual interdependency can start to feel overly restrictive. Most couples gradually find their way to a more mature interdependence that retains some of the intensity of their initial connection while making room for each person to be more fully him or herself. It is this transition that is problematic for many couples.

Women are socialized to anticipate, and practice all of their lives to be in an intimate relationship, so their response to the intensity of the initial connection in the honeymoon phase is to want more. Men, who are less experienced in relationships and less confident, find it easier to be more emotionally present and available for connection in the early stages of a relationship when they are hungrier for connection (even though they might think of it as being hungry for sex) and are more willing to stretch beyond their usual comfort zone to get that early connection. As the relationship develops, and women do a wonderful job helping men feel more secure, men become less scared about being abandoned and start to pull back to what is a more familiar and comfortable level of emotional connection for them. Remember, the intimacy that women crave is often threatening to men. Women pursue their partners because people in a one-down position have little choice but to push for change. Men withdraw because the person in the more privileged position has every reason to resist change.

Men's emotional withdrawal is very disappointing to women, either because they were initially getting the kind of connection they wanted in a relationship, or because they were getting enough of that connection to believe in (or convince themselves of) their partner's potential for more. In either case, their partner is no longer giving them as much of what they want in a relationship, and they know that he is capable of more. It can feel like a bait and switch to women, like their partner only gave what them what they wanted as long as they played "hard to get," and as soon as he got what he wanted, he started to withdraw. Sadly, women often learn that the more fully they are themselves the more likely their partners are to be intimidated. In response, women learn to diminish themselves, to be less fully who they are.[242] As one woman in my office put it, "there is a lot of who I want to be, but if I'm fully me it doesn't work in this relationship."

Women learn pretty quickly that the most effective ways to get their partners to emotionally reengage is either to withhold the reassurance they normally provide, and/or to escalate their level of emotional distress. Both of these strategies can be effective because they reactivate men's fears, which lead men to do an about face and start leaning back into the relationship.

The problem is that both of these strategies are often experienced by men as critical. Feeling criticized is one of the complaints I hear most often expressed by men about their relationships. Sometimes I can see the criticism men are experiencing, and other times I really have to strain to understand how they heard their partners as critical. While men may be overly sensitive to criticism from their partner, they are not just imagining it. The truth is that women often do feel critical of men at this stage in a relationship. Since they don't understand that their partner is scared, they are most likely to interpret his behavior as a punishment. They are angry at their partner for withdrawing, for giving them a taste of what they want and then pulling it back.

Whether their partner intended to be critical or not, when men hear their partners as critical, they tend to respond by being defensive, which is the second communication style that is problematic in a relationship. Men tend to get very rational and concrete and to argue with their partner about the specifics of their complaints, rather than being able to hear or respond to the underlying request for greater connection. They get defensive because the emotion between them escalates to levels that are threatening to men and so they get rational and concrete in an effort to bring the conversation down to a level of emotion that feels less threatening.

As you can imagine, or know from your own experience, men's defensive withdrawal escalates things even further in the couple because it means that women get even less of the connection they want. The problem with withdrawal as a protective strategy is the same problem with using drugs and alcohol to regulate your mood. Both are quite effective initially, but over time it takes more and more of the same strategies to produce the same desired effect, to the point where these strategies not only become largely ineffective but counter-productive. Each partner's defenses escalate the reactions of the other, resulting in an escalating cycle of increasing conflict and decreasing intimacy that is familiar to so many couples.

Women may then escalate their criticisms to the level of contempt, which is the strongest predictor of relationship dissatisfaction. Many women grew up in families in which they saw their mothers resort to contempt with their fathers, after having exhausted every effort to engage him emotionally. In response, men often escalate their defensiveness to stonewalling, also having observed their fathers' resorting to this extreme defense after exhausting their efforts to engage with their partners in a way that did not overwhelm them with fears.

The good news is that while it takes two people to create these destructive patterns, either partner can change those patterns just by doing his or her part differently. Intimate relationships tend to trigger us into reenacting unresolved childhood issues. This is why going back to visit family can be so wonderful and distressing at the same time. However, if either partner is willing to do his or her part differently, an opportunity is created for things to go better for the couple.

Family therapist Carl Whitaker said that the key to a successful marriage happens in those moments when you are in a horrible fight with your spouse and are completely convinced that everything she is saying is just crazy and has absolutely no merit, and that you are one-hundred percent in the right.[243] There are three possibilities in that moment. Either you believe that your partner is psychotic and is not capable of recognizing the difference between reality and fantasy, or that she is malevolent and intentionally trying to hurt you, or you push yourself to do the work to recognize the truth in what she is saying.

For men, the work is to forgo their familiar protections of defensiveness and stonewalling. A relatively simple thing that men can do (simple, but not easy) to be less defensive is to work on taking responsibility for their behavior. Jewish ethics teaches us that we are all responsible for the impact of our words, whether the impact is what we intended or not.[244] It is a radically transformative practice to set aside your automatic defensive rebuttals in order to be able to listen to another person speak about the impact of your behavior on them. Often nothing else is required—not an apology, or any corrective action. Sometimes the simple act of non-defensive listening can itself be transformative.

One of the most effective ways for men to learn how to be less defensive is to work on becoming more comfortable with the interdependency of intimacy and less afraid of conflict in their relationships. Boys start out just as attached to their early caregivers and childhood friends as women are. When men lose the close relationships of their youth they suffer horribly.[245] Men's choice to pursue the external power represented by their fathers at the cost of being able to give freely and receive love results in an atrophied development, both emotionally and interpersonally, which creates a love-hate relationship with intimacy. Men are scared of women because they are not at all confident of being loved for who they are, and they worry that the love they receive is conditionally dependent on all of the caretaking they do. No amount of reassurance from their partner is likely to change that as long as they continue to feel insecure about how deserving of love they truly are. Accordingly, for men to become less afraid of women in their intimate relationships, ultimately they are going to need to become more fluent and proficient in intimacy.

For men to get better at intimacy they must relinquish some of the privilege inherent in the withdrawn, avoidant defenses they've utilized and allow themselves to be more aware of, and then risk acknowledging, some of their own emotional dependency and need for intimate connection. Men need to learn that although their withdrawal is initially effective in reducing their level of emotional distress, over time it creates enough distress in their partner to escalate her emotional reactivity, which is exactly what men were trying to manage to begin with.

In order to learn not to use withdrawal as a defense, men also need to learn to become more comfortable with conflict in their relationships and learn to see conflict as an opportunity to connect rather than as a threat so that their fear of conflict doesn't trigger their fears of abandonment and lead them to withdraw. Since men superficially misunderstand conflict with their partners as a behavioral problem, they tend to seek behavioral solutions, typically starting with an apology. Apologies are not generally effective relationship repair, because they are most often a thinly veiled attempt to prematurely bring the argument to a close and stop their partner from being angry in order to restore the status quo without ever giving a full hearing to their partner's feelings. These false apologies often avoid the courage to really look within in an effort to understand your part of a conflict, and they do not include a genuine expression of empathy for the impact of your behavior on your partner. They are simply a defensive maneuver, designed to get your partner off your back. The real message is not "I'm sorry," but is "please stop being angry at me."

The first step when your partner is hurt is to let her know that you understand how she feels on her terms, not yours. This is not just a matter of repeating back to her what she said. Men sometimes get angry and frustrated when parroting back their partners' words doesn't smooth things over, complaining "but I am listening to you!" One of the biggest mistakes men make in relationships is stopping there. Nobody feels heard or knows that you care if you just repeat back what they said to you. You also have to listen between the lines, using your empathy and intuition to go beyond the concrete words and get to the deeper sense of what she is trying to tell you.

As you listen to your partner, think of yourself as an anthropologist learning about a culture you don't know anything about. Jung is purported to have recommended that therapists approach every psychotherapy session as if they had never done psychotherapy before, what Buddhists refer to as "beginners mind." When new therapists tell me that they are getting bored, I suggest that they try listening harder.

Be curious about your partner's experience. Ask her questions about what it is like for her. Try as much as possible to refrain from your own judgments or assumptions about her experience, and listen to understand what she's saying on her terms Strive for a sense of knowing what her experience was like from the inside. I can assure you that you will be much more interested in what your partner has to say, and she will most likely feel deeply seen and cared for.

The second and more important step, and the one that people sadly often leave out, is to take responsibility for the impact of your behavior. This does not mean saying you were wrong. It's not about right or wrong. It's about acknowledging that you understand how your behavior has impacted someone you love. Whether or not you meant to hurt her is much less important, and falling back on that is just a way to dodge acknowledging that you hurt someone.

Your partner needs to know that hurting her matters to you, that you have some personal reaction to her being hurt, and that it has some impact on you. You have to be willing to put a little skin in the game, dig a little deeper inside yourself and share with her some of how you are feeling in response to her feelings. This is what empathy is.

Lastly, you have to be willing to give her some realistic indication of what you are willing to do to decrease the likelihood of hurting her again this way in the future. Don't promise you won't do it again because you almost certainly will. Most of the significant hurts in couples come from people acting out their own deeply ingrained characterological patterns. Much as you might try, it is highly unlikely that you are going to be able to change that overnight. It is not a measure of how much you care about someone, but of how deeply ingrained these patterns are. We unconsciously choose a partner precisely because he or she is likely to play out these exact same patterns that are so hurtful to us. What you can offer is some realistic understanding of where this behavior is coming from for you, and what kind of internal work you are willing to do to be more understanding and more sensitive to the impact of your behavior on your partner.

Men tend to escalate to the defense of stonewalling when they are emotionally flooded and feel they need to take drastic action to protect themselves. Men can work on this by learning how to more effectively soothe themselves when they are emotionally overloaded. This is where individual therapy can be very helpful, as is having other men to call who can help you soothe yourself so that you can reengage productively in the relationship.

Just as men need to relinquish the privilege that comes from withdrawing from conflict, women need to learn how to refrain from using the destructive defenses of criticism and contempt. Women understanding the core role that men's fears of women play in their intimate relationships helps women have more empathy and compassion for their partners, and to be less reactive to the destructive defenses that men often use, which in turn should lead to more intimacy, which is what women want and men need.

Women can learn to be less aggressive in their pursuit of contact, and to pay more attention to how it is going with their partner and make appropriate mid-course corrections. Pushing hard with someone who is scared just leads to more withdrawal from him, and pain for both of you. When women are hurt or disappointed with their partner, it goes much better if she can talk about her feelings without blaming or indicting her partner for the failings that led to her disappointment.

One woman who participated in a multiple-day workshop for men and women on men's fears of women wrote:

> *I jumped at the chance to join a group of men and women coming together to explore men's fear of intimacy with women in relationships, myself desperate to find answers to seemingly intractable dynamics in my marriage. . . In this process a space of love and empathy opened for each other in our shared vulnerabilities and fears. I fell in love with each of the men in turn, for their honesty, for their courage to share the raw experience of their frustrations and pain in their own marriages. I went home reflecting not only on what my husband's experiences might be with me, but I think just as importantly, with a clearer insight into the subtle ways in which I blame and withhold and stand my guard, even sabotage, because of my own fears of intimacy and deeply held resentments. This led me to make subtle shifts, to consciously open more, to understand his unspoken pain from a non-defensive place. I began to share more of my own fears. Our relationship softened noticeably. He noticed. I believe*

it would have taken months, if not years, of couple's therapy for me to let go of my intransigence.

In working toward being less critical of their partners, another thing that women can do is to learn to forgo the enabling they do when they "help" their partners. I put the word "help" in quotation marks to recognize that these well-intentioned efforts to help are a double-edged sword that can hurt as much as they help. Women "help" their partners because that's often the only way they know to get some of what they need for themselves and their families. Women want to feel cared about and know that they are important to their partners, so they "help" their partners by reminding them repeatedly of the dates of their anniversary and her birthday. They send links to gifts she wants to spare him the anxiety that comes with having no idea of what to get her and spare herself another year of disappointment. Women want to feel closer to their partners and more satisfied in their sexual relationship, but they are afraid that if they try to talk about their own sexual desires and preferences they will make their partner feel inadequate and defensive, so they "help" their partners by exaggerating their sexual passion during lovemaking. Women want a partner who is a devoted parent and are often frustrated by their partner's repeated failures to show up and be engaged with their children, so they "help" by intervening with the kids to smooth things over when their father disappoints them or behaves badly.

Women are often aware of the ways in which they "help," and they are often resigned to getting their needs met in these indirect ways after repeatedly being met with withdrawal and stonewalling when they try to talk more directly to their partners. Men, on the other hand, are largely unaware of the ways in which their partners "help" them. Their partners "help" them so seamlessly that men come to take it for granted and don't even notice it, leaving their partners even more resentful. Men typically are unaware of how much "help" they are getting until conflict between them reaches the level where their partner starts to withdraw some of the "help" she has always offered or threatens to withdraw it all together.

When a relationship has devolved to the point of contempt or stonewalling, the journey back can be daunting, but as Lao Tzu said, "a journey of a thousand miles begins with a single step." In this case, those single steps consist of acts of appreciation and validation. I have been observing what makes long term relationships successful for decades, and what I've concluded is that it is simple acts of kindness and validation, simple gestures that let your partner know that you know who she is and that she matters to you. Gottman's research confirms that it takes five positive interactions to counteract one negative one and keep a relationship on track.[246]

In the television show *This is Us*,[247] Miguel tells his best friend Jack that he and his wife are divorcing because they "stopped noticing each other." Miguel explains that he started every day of their relationship by making coffee for his wife, just the way she liked it, and bringing it to her in bed. One day he woke up, made himself coffee, but just didn't feel like making a cup for his wife, and so he didn't. Miguel says, "The worst part is she didn't even notice. We stopped noticing each other. We stopped trying to make each other happy. When we realized that, we knew it was over." It may seem that not bringing your partner a cup of coffee isn't much of a reason for divorce, but I believe that each cup of coffee that Miguel brought his wife was the kind of critical act of validation and reassurance that was keeping their marriage alive.

Relationships start to go bad not necessarily because there is an increase in conflict. It is just as likely to be because couples stop validating and reassuring each other that they are loved and important to each other. Remember that in the Still Face experiments the boy babies were more distressed by their mother's emotional withdrawal than were the girls.[248] When this kind of emotional withdrawal happens in adult relationships, men are less equipped to tolerate it than women.

We like to think of ourselves as being essentially self-contained, secure, and not needing this kind of reassurance from anyone. The truth is that we all need it a lot more than we let ourselves or anyone else know. Being in an intimate relationship with someone is one of the riskiest, most vulnerable things we can do. Being intimate with someone means that you will inevitably and repeatedly be hurt in ways that you could never even imagine when you were alone. For men, it recreates the early fears of abandonment they experienced with their mothers.

As a man, you can learn to tolerate this vulnerability by practicing acts of kindness and reassurance on a regular basis. To start with, learn how to be more proactive about, and take more responsibility for, maintaining good connection in your relationships. This might not come naturally to you, not having had much practice when you were younger. I've even had some guys write down on their to daily do list, "appreciate my wife." Try not letting a day go by without doing something to let your partner know that you are thinking about her, love her, and appreciate how much better your life is with her.

Couples generally find it easier and more enjoyable to be generous with each other in these ways early in their relationship. Over time, however, a series of resentments, feelings left over from conflicts they have not been able to resolve on their own, can lead to a mutual withholding of this critical reassurance. As Miguel said, they stop noticing each other. Men in particular often withhold this kind of reassurance from their partners because they have been socialized to fear being controlled by women and to think of loving acts of kindness as not manly, something women coerce men to do. The couple may think of their mutual withholding as a series of petty retributions, not understanding that their accumulation can threaten the trust that is essential for their marriage.

When you and your partner fall out of the habit of spontaneously reassuring each other, you both need to learn how to find your way back to each other in a more intentional, deliberate way. This will feel awkward at first, but you each need to learn how to do this in a more conscious, deliberate way when it is no longer happening spontaneously. Equally important, you need to learn how to be intentional about expressing your appreciation for the reassurance you are receiving from your partner. Often times I see the healing process in couples fall flat when one person takes a risk to be more open or intimate, and their partner doesn't reciprocate simply because it's been so long that she has learned to protect herself by not noticing all of the disappointing, hurtful interactions. She simply did not notice that her partner was doing something different this time. If you like what you are receiving from your partner, slather on the appreciation. Dog trainers say that the most common mistake people make is not giving their pet nearly enough treats. I frequently remind people that it is nearly impossible to overdo love and appreciation. There is no known toxic limit on expressions of love and affirmation.

# # #

ENDNOTES

1. O'Neil, J. M. (1981a). Male sex-role conflicts, sexism, and masculinity: Implications for men, women, and the counseling psychologist. The Counseling Psychologist, 9, 61-80.

2. O'Neil, J. M. (1981b). Patterns of gender role conflict and strain: Sexism and fear of femininity in men's lives. The Personnel and Guidance Journal, 60, 203-210.

3. O'Neil, J. M. (1982). Gender role conflict and strain in men's lives: Implications for psychiatrists, psychologists, and other human service providers. In K. Solomon & N. Levy (Eds.), Men in transition: Theory and therapy. Plenum Publishing Company.

4. O'Neil, J.M. (2008). Summarizing twenty-five years of research on men's gender role conflict using the Gender Role Conflict Scale: New research paradigms and clinical implications. The Counseling Psychologist. 36, 358-445.

5. O'Neil, J.M. (2008). Men's gender role conflict: 25-year research summary (Special Issue). The Counseling Psychologist, 36, 358-476.

6. O'Neil, J.M. (2015) Men's gender role conflict: Psychological costs, consequences, and an agenda for change. American Psychological Association.

7. O'Neil, J.M. & Denke, R. (2015). An Empirical review of the gender role conflict research: New conceptual models and research paradigms. In J. Wong and S. Wester (Eds.) APA Handbook of the Psychology of Men and Masculinities. (pp 51-80), APA Books.

8. Adler, A. (1927). Understanding human nature. Garden City Publishing Company.

9. Boehm, F. (1930). The femininity-complex in men. International Journal of Psychoanalysis, 11, 444-469.

10. Freud, S. (1937). Analysis terminable and interminable. In P. Rieff (Ed.), Freud: Therapy and technique pp. 233-271). Macmillan.

11. Horney, K. (1932). The dread of women. *International Journal of Psychoanalysis, 13*, 348-360.

12. Jung, K. (1953). *Animus and anima.* Collected Works, vol. 7, Pantheon.

13. Lederer, W. (1968). The fear of women. Harcourt, Brace, Jovanovich.

14. O'Neil, J.M. (2015) Men's gender role conflict: Psychological costs, consequences, and an agenda for change. American Psychological Association.

15. O'Neil, J. M., & Egan, J. (1992). Men and women's gender role journeys: A metaphor for healing, transition, and transformation. In B. Wainrib (Ed.)

Gender issues across the life cycle. Springer Publishing Co.

16. O'Neil, J. M., Egan, J., Owen, S.V., & Murry, V.M. (1993). The gender role journey measure (JRJM): Scale development and psychometric evaluations. Sex Roles,28, 167-185.

17. Glick, P., & Fiske, S. T. (1996). The ambivalent sexism inventory: Differentiating hostile and benevolent sexism. Journal of personality and social psychology, 70(3), 491.

18. Guttentag, M., & Secord, P. F. (1983). *Too many women: The Sex Ration Question*. Sage Publications, Inc.

19. Kelley, H. H., & Thibaut, J. W. (1978). *Interpersonal relations: A Theory of Interdependence*. New York: John Wiley & Sons.

20. Chen, Z., Fiske, S. T., & Lee, T. L. (2009). Ambivalent sexism and power-related gender-role ideology in marriage. *Sex roles*, *60*(11-12), 765-778.

21. Glick, P., & Fiske, S. T. (1996). The ambivalent sexism inventory: Differentiating hostile and benevolent sexism. *Journal of personality and social psychology*, *70*(3), 491.

22. Herrera, M. C., Expósito, F., & Moya, M. (2012). Negative reactions of men to the loss of power in gender relations: Lilith vs. Eve. *The European Journal of Psychology Applied to Legal Context*, *4*(1), 17.

23. Glick, P., & Fiske, S. T. (1996). The ambivalent sexism inventory: Differentiating hostile and benevolent sexism. *Journal of personality and social psychology*, *70*(3), 491.

24. Ibid

25. Weiss, A. G. (2018). Men's Anger Might Mask Fear: I Know You're Mad but You Might Also be Scared. *From Fear to Intimacy* https://www.psychologytoday.com/us/blog/fear-intimacy/201809/mens-anger-might-mask-fear.

26. Cohen, R. (2015). Welcome to the manosphere: A brief guide to the controversial men's rights movement. Retrieved April 6, 2019, from https://www.motherjones.com/politics/2015/01/manosphere-mens-rights-movement-terms/.

27. Jordan, J., Kaplan, A., Stiver, I., Surrey, J., Miller, J. (1991). *Women's growth in connection: Writings from the Stone Center*. Guilford press.

28. American Psychological Association, B. A. M. G. G. (2/9/19). APA guidelines for psychological practice with boys and men. http://www.apa.org/about/policy/psychological-practice-boys-men-guidelines.pdg.

29. Kaufman, M. (1994). *Cracking the Armour*. Penguin.

30. Hotline, N. D. V. 50 Obstacles to Leaving: 1-10. Retrieved March 31, 2019, from https://www.thehotline.org/2013/06/10/50-obstacles-to-leaving-1-10/.

31. Hayak, S. (2017). Harvey Weinstein Is My Monster Too. *New York Times*.

32. Corsini, R. (2016). *The Dictionary of Psychology*. Routledge.

33. Ducat, S. (2005). *The Wimp Factor: Gender Gaps, Holy Wars, and the Politics of Anxious Masculinity* (1st ed.). Beacon Press.

34. Tronick, E., Als, H., Adamson, L., Wise, S., & Brazelton, T. B. (1978). The infant's response to entrapment between contradictory messages in face-to-face interaction. *Journal of the American Academy of Child psychiatry*, *17*(1), 1-13.

35. Weinberg, M. K., Tronick, E. Z., Cohn, J. F., & Olson, K. L. (1999). Gender differences in emotional expressivity and self-regulation during early infancy. *Developmental psychology*, *35*(1), 175.

36. Centers for Disease Control and Prevention. (2001). (2001), National Intimate Partner and Sexual Violence Survey, United States.

37. Kimmel, M. S. (2004). Masculinity as homophobia: Fear, shame, and silence in the construction of gender identity. *Race, class, and gender in the United States: An integrated study*, *81*, 93.

38. Kierski, W., & Blazina, C. (2010). The male fear of the feminine and its effects on counseling and psychotherapy. *The Journal of Men's Studies*, *17*(2), 155-172.

39. Barkhorn, E. (2013). Are successful women really less likable than successful men. *The Atlantic*. March 14.

40. Lederer, W. (1968). *The Fear of Women: An Inquiry Into the Enigma of Women and Why Men Through the Ages Have Both Loved and Dreaded Her.* New York: Harcourt, Brace Jovanovich.

41. Ibid

42. Landau, M. J., Goldenberg, J. L., Greenberg, J., Gillath, O., Solomon, S., Cox, C. (2006). The siren's call: Terror management and the threat of men's sexual attraction to women. *Journal of personality and social psychology*, *90*(1), 129.

43. *Ibid*

44. Ibid

45. Campbell, J. (1968). *Creative Mythology.* New York: Viking Press.

46. Glick, P., & Fiske, S. T. (1996). The ambivalent sexism inventory: Differentiating hostile and benevolent sexism. *Journal of personality and social psychology*, *70*(3), 491.

47. Lederer, W. (1968). *The Fear of Women: An Inquiry Into the Enigma of Women and Why Men Through the Ages Have Both Loved and Dreaded Her.* New York: Harcourt, Brace Jovanovich.

48. Hays, H. R. (1964). *The dangerous sex: The Myth of Feminie Evil*. New York: G.P. Putnam's Sons.

49. Dinnerstein, D. (1999). *The Mermaid and the Minotaur.* New York: Other Books.

50. Lederer, W. (1968). *The Fear of Women: An Inquiry Into the Enigma of Women and Why Men Through the Ages Have Both Loved and Dreaded Her.* New York: Harcourt, Brace Jovanovich.

51. Horney, K. (1932). Observations on a Specific Difference in the Dread Felt by Men and by Women Respectively for the Opposite Sex. *International Journal of Psychoanalysis*, *13*, 348-360.

52. Lederer, W. (1968). *The Fear of Women: An Inquiry Into the Enigma of Women and Why Men Through the Ages Have Both Loved and Dreaded Her.* New York: Harcourt, Brace Jovanovich.

53. Wiesner, M. (1993). *Women and Gender in Early Modern Europe.* Cambridge, England: Cambridge University Press.

54. Lea, H. C. (1961). *A History of the Inquisition of the Middle Ages.* New York: Macmillan.

55. Ducat, S. (2005). *The Wimp Factor: Gender Gaps, Holy Wars, and the Politics of Anxious Masculinity* (1st ed.). Beacon Press.

56. Bederman, G. *Manliness and Civilization: A Cultural History of Gender and Race in the United States. Chicago:Cited in Ducat, S. (1995) The Wimp Factor.* Boston: Beacon Press.

57. Rotundo, A. *American Manhood: Transformations in Masculinity From the Revolution to the Modern Era.*

Cited in Ducat, S. (1995) The Wimp Factor. Boston: Beacon Press.

58. Carnes, M. (1989). *Secret Ritual and Manhood in Victorian America*. New Haven, CT: Yale University Press.

59. Clover, C. J. (2015). *Men, Women, and Chain Saws: Gender in the Modern Horror Film-Updated Edition* (15). Princeton University Press.

60. *Ibid*

61. Shakespeare, W. (2001). *Hamlet*. Classic Books Company.

62. Butler, S. (1759). *The Geunuine Remains in Verse and Prose of Mr. Samuel Butler, Author of* Hudibras. (II). London: Toson, in the Strang.

63. Burr, B. Retrieved September 17, 2017, from https://www.youtube.com/watch?list=RDspinaW-zC-E&v=kk5iqoYVUQc.

64. Jack, D. C. (1993). *Silencing The Self.* Harper Collins.

65. Horsmon, S. 21 Things Unhappy Husbands are Afraid to Say Out Loud. Retrieved March 18, 2018, from https://goodmenproject.com/marriage-2/21-things-unhappy-husbands-are-afraid-to-say-out-loud-stvhn/.

66. (2002). My Big Fat Greek Wedding. https://www.youtube.com/watch?v=8fJoPI-xytM.

67. Archer, J. (2000). Sex differences in aggression between heterosexual partners: A meta-analytic review. *Psychological bulletin*, *126*(5), 651.

68. Bates, E. A., Graham-Kevan, N., & Archer, J. (2014). Testing predictions from the male control theory of men's partner violence. *Aggressive behavior*, *40*(1), 42-55.

69. Smith, B. (2019). 10 Signs You're Whipped. Retrieved April 26, 2019, from https://www.mensfitness.com/women/dating-advice/10-signs-youre-whipped.

70. Coombs, R. H. (1991). Marital status and personal well-being: A literature review. *Family relations*, *40*(1), 97-102.

71. Radloff, L. (1975). Sex differences in depression: The Effects of Occupation on Marital Status. *Sex roles*, *1*(3), 249-265.

72. Campbell, A. (1981). *The Sense of Well-Being in America: Recent Patterns and Trends*. New York: McGraw Hill.

73. Gurin, G., Veroff, J., & Feld, S. (1960). Americans view their mental health: A nationwide interview survey. Basic Books.

74. Cashion, B. E. (1970). Durkheim's Concept of Anomie and It's Relationship to Divorce. *Sociology and Social Research*, *55*, 72-81.

75. Gove, W. R., & Tudor, J. F. (1973). Adult sex roles and mental illness. *American journal of Sociology*, *78*(4), 812-835.

76. Hogendoorn, B., Leopold, T., & Bol, T. (2020). Divorce and diverging poverty rates: A risk-and-

vulnerability approach. *Journal of Marriage and Family*, *82*(3), 1089-1109.

77. Shpancer, N. (2015). Is Marriage Worth the Trouble for Women? The Benefits Go Mostly to Men. Retrieved March 12, 2017, from https://www.psychologytoday.com/us/blog/insight-therapy/201510/is-marriage-worth-the-trouble-women.

78. Goodwin, P. (2009). *Who Marries and When?: Age at First Marriage in the United States, 2002* ((19)). US Department of Health and Human Services, Centers for Disease Control and Prevention.

79. Autor, D., Dorn, D., & Hanson, G. (2018). When work disappears: Manufacturing decline and the falling marriage-market value of young men. *American Economic Review: Insights*.

80. Shpancer, N. (2015). Is Marriage Worth the Trouble for Women? The Benefits Go Mostly to Men. Retrieved March 12, 2017, from https://www.psychologytoday.com/us/blog/insight-therapy/201510/is-marriage-worth-the-trouble-women.

81. Weiss, A. G. (2002). The lost role of dependency in psychotherapy. *Gestalt Review*, *6*(1), 6-17.

82. Weiss, A. G. (2021). *Living and Loving Mutually: How to Break Free from Hurtful Relationship Patterns*. Lasting Impact Press.

83. Erikson, E. H. (1994). *Identity: Youth and Crisis*. W. W. Norton & Company.

84. Levinson, D. J. (1978). *The Seasons of a Man's Life*. Random House Digital, Inc.

85. Stiver, I. (1991). The Meanings of "Dependency" in female-male relationships. In Jordan, J., Kaplan, A., Stiver, I. (Ed.), *Women's Growth in Connection: Writings from the Stone Center*. New York: Guilford.

86. Weiss, A. G. (2021). *Living and Loving Mutually: How to Break Free from Hurtful Relationship Patterns*. Lasting Impact Press.

87. Pollak, S., & Gilligan, C. (1982). Images of violence in Thematic Apperception Test stories. *Journal of Personality and Social psychology*, *42*(1), 159.

88. Oluo, I. (10/14/16). Men, You Can Survive Without Us - Please Try. https://theestablishment.co/men-you-can-survive-without-us-please-try-19352ada1b05/.

89. Zinczenko, D., & Spiker, T. (2007). *Men, Love & Sex*. Rodale.

90. Elam, P. (10/17/16). What Men Fear Most. https://avoiceformen.com/featured/what-men-fear-most/.

91. Dinnerstein, D. (1999). *The Mermaid and the Minotaur*. New York: Other Books.

92. Miller, A. (1997). *The Drama of the Gifted Child*. Basic Books.

93. Freud, S. (1921). *The Interpretation of Dreams*. George Allen & Unwin.

94. Adams, R. (9/22/14). Study Finds that 'Happy Wife, Happy Life' is Pretty Dead On. Retrieved May 19, 2019, from https://www.huffpost.com/entry/happy-wife-happy-life_n_5843596.

95. Weiss, A. G. (2020). Who Gets Up in the Middle of the Night in Your House? Power Struggles Between Men and Women About Anxiety https://www.psychologytoday.com/us/blog/fear-intimacy/202009/who-gets-in-the-middle-the-night-in-your-house.

96. Chapman, G. (2014). *The 5 Love Languages for Men*. Moody Publishers.

97. Weiss, A. G. (2002). The lost role of dependency in psychotherapy. *Gestalt Review*, *6*(1), 6-17.

98. May, C. (2017). Are Women More Emotionally Expressive than Men? Retrieved June 9, 2019, from https://www.scientificamerican.com/article/are-women-more-emotionally-expressive-than-men/?redirect=1.

99. Gray, J. (1993). *Men Are from Mars, Women Are from Venus*. Harper Collins.

100. Wester, S. R., Vogel, D. L., Pressly, P. K., & Heesacker, M. (2002). Sex differences in emotion: A critical review of the literature and implications for counseling psychology. *The Counseling Psychologist*, *30*(4), 630-652.

101. Rivers, C., & Barnett, R. (2013). *The Truth About Girls and Boys: Challenging Toxic Stereotypes About Our Children* (Reprint ed.). Columbia University Press.

102. Remes, O., Brayne, C., Van Der Linde, R., & Lafortune, L. (2016). A systematic review of reviews on the prevalence of anxiety disorders in adult populations. *Brain and behavior*, *6*(7).

103. Felder, R. (1986). Personal communication.

104. Gilligan, C. (1977). In a different voice: Women's conceptions of self and of morality. *Harvard educational review*, *47*(4), 481-517.

105. Joiner, T. (2011). *Lonely at the Top*. St. Martin's Press.

106. Landau, M. J., Goldenberg, J. L., Greenberg, J., Gillath, O., Solomon, S., Cox, C. et al. (2006). The siren's call: Terror management and the threat of men's sexual attraction to women. *Journal of personality and social psychology*, *90*(1), 129.

107. Diamond, J. (2017). The one thing men want more than sex. *Good Men Project.*

108. Fisher, T. D., Moore, Z. T., & Pittenger, M.-J. (2012). Sex on the brain?: An examination of frequency of sexual cognitions as a function of gender, erotophilia, and social desirability. *Journal of Sex Research*, *49*(1), 69-77.

109. Jones, M. (2/11/18). When Porn is Sex Ed.

110. DeAngelo, D. (03/25/21). Ten Most Dangerous Mistakes Men Make with Women. https://www.nairaland.com/89759/ten-most-dangerous-mistakes-men.

111. Diamond, J. (2017). The one thing men want more than sex. *Good Men Project.*

112. Ogas, O., & Gaddam, S. (2011). *A billion wicked thoughts: What the world's largest experiment reveals about human desire.* Dutton/Penguin Books.

113. Chadwick, S. B., & van Anders, S. M. (2017). Do women's orgasms function as a masculinity achievement for men. *The Journal of sex research, 54*(9), 1141-1152.

114. Ley, D. (2017). Why He Cares About Your Orgasm: Research Sheds Light on Men's Motivations for Giving Pleasure. https://www.psychologytoday.com/us/blog/women-who-stray/201703/why-he-cares-about-your-orgasm.

115. Perel, E. (2007). *Mating in Captivity*. Harper Collins.

116. Ibid, p. 161

117. Graham, C. A., Mercer, C. H., Tanton, C., Jones, K. G., Johnson, A. M., Wellings, K. et al. (2017). What factors are associated with reporting lacking interest in sex and how do these vary by gender? Findings from the third British national survey of sexual attitudes and lifestyles. BMJ open, 7(9).

118. Morris, D. (1968). The Naked Ape: A Zoologist'study of the Human Animal. Cape.

119. Piaget, J., & Inhelder, B. (2008). *The Psychology Of The Child.*

120. Tronick, E., Als, H., Adamson, L., Wise, S., & Brazelton, T. B. (1978). The infant's response to entrapment between contradictory messages in face-to-face interaction. *Journal of the American Academy of Child psychiatry*, *17*(1), 1-13.

121. Bareket, O., Kahalon, R., Shnabel, N., & Glick, P. (2018). The Madonna-Whore Dichotomy: Men who perceive women's nurturance and sexuality as mutually exclusive endorse patriarchy and show lower relationship satisfaction. *Sex Roles*, *79*(9), 519-532.

122. Appleby, D. W., & Palkovitz, R. (2007). Factors influencing a divorced father's involvement with his children. Liberty University.

123. Ducat, S. (2005). *The Wimp Factor: Gender Gaps, Holy Wars, and the Politics of Anxious Masculinity* (1st ed.). Beacon Press.

124. Wilkerson, I. (2020). *Caste*. Penguin Random House.

125. *Ibid*, p. 11

126. Vandello, J. A., Bosson, J. K., Cohen, D., Burnaford, R. M., & Weaver, J. R. (2008). Precarious manhood. *Journal of personality and social psychology*, *95*(6), 1325.

127. Gilmore, D. D. (1990). *Manhood in the Making*. Yale University Press. Cited in Vandello, 2008.

128. Beinart, P. (2016). Fear of a female president. *The Atlantic*, *15*.

129. Levy, G. D., Taylor, M. G., & Gelman, S. A. (1995). Traditional and evaluative aspects of flexibility in gender roles, social conventions, moral rules, and physical laws. *Child development*, *66*(2), 515-531.

130. Perel, E. (2007). *Mating in Captivity*. Harper Collins.

131. Kimmel, M. S. (2004). Masculinity as homophobia: Fear, shame, and silence in the construction of gender identity. *Race, class, and gender in the United States: An integrated study*, *81*, 93.

132. Jung, C. G. (2014). *The Archetypes and the Collective Unconscious*. Routledge.

133. Felder, R. E., & Weiss, A. G. (1991). *Experiential Psychotherapy*. University Press of America.

134. Weiss, A. (2015). Experiential Psychotherapy. In E. Neukrug (Ed.), *The Sage Encyclopedia of Theory in Counseling and Psychotherapy*. Sage.

135. Maccoby, E. E. (1988). Gender as a social category. *Developmental Psychology*, *24*, 755-765.

136. Fiske, A. P., Haslam, N., & Fiske, S. T. (1991). Confusing one person with another: What errors reveal about the elementary forms of social relations. *Journal of personality and social psychology*, *60*(5), 656.

137. Banaji, M. R., & Prentice, D. A. (1994). The self in social contexts. *Annual review of psychology*, *45*(1), 297-332.

138. Shutts, K., Kenward, B., Falk, H., Ivegran, A., & Fawcett, C. (2017). Early preschool environments and

gender: Effects of gender pedagogy in Sweden. *Journal of experimental child psychology*, *162*, 1-17.

139. Rivers, C., & Barnett, R. (2013). *The Truth About Girls and Boys: Challenging Toxic Stereotypes About Our Children* (Reprint ed.). Columbia University Press.

140. Lytton, H., & Romney, D. M. (1991). Parents' differential socialization of boys and girls: A meta-analysis. *Psychological bulletin*, *109*(2), 267.

141. Kosciw, J. G., Greytak, E. A., Bartkiewicz, M. J., Boesen, M. J., & Palmer, N. A. (2012). *The 2011 National School Climate Survey: The Experiences of Lesbian, Gay, Bisexual and Transgender Youth in Our Nation's Schools.* ERIC.

142. Shutts, K., Kenward, B., Falk, H., Ivegran, A., & Fawcett, C. (2017). Early preschool environments and gender: Effects of gender pedagogy in Sweden. *Journal of experimental child psychology*, *162*, 1-17.

143. Kaufman, M. (1994). *Cracking the Armour*. Penguin.

144. Levy, G. D., Taylor, M. G., & Gelman, S. A. (1995). Traditional and evaluative aspects of flexibility in gender roles, social conventions, moral rules, and physical laws. *Child development*, *66*(2), 515-531.

145. O'Neil, J. M. (2014). *Men's Gender Role Conflict*. Amer Psychological Assn.

146. Jack, D. C. (1993). *Silencing The Self*. Harper Collins.

147. O'Neil, J. M. (2014). *Men's Gender Role Conflict*. Amer Psychological Assn.

148. Borthick, M. J. (1998). Gender role conflict and suicidal ideation in an adolescent and young adult population: Age 18-24 years. *Dissertation Abstracts International*, *58*, 18-24.

149. Springer, K. W., & Mouzon, D. M. (2011). "Macho men" and preventive health care: Implications for older men in different social classes. *Journal of Health and Social Behavior*, *52*(2), 212-227.

150. Yousaf, O., Popat, A., & Hunter, M. S. (2015). An investigation of masculinity attitudes, gender, and attitudes toward psychological help-seeking. *Psychology of Men & Masculinity*, *16*(2), 234.

151. Mahalik, J. R., Aldarondo, E., Gilbert-Gokhale, S., & Shore, E. (2005). The role of insecure attachment and gender role stress in predicting controlling behaviors in men who batter. *Journal of Interpersonal Violence*, *20*(5), 617-631.

152. Springer, K. W., Lee, C., & Carr, D. (2019). Spousal Breadwinning Across 30 Years of Marriage and Husbands' Health: A Gendered Life Course Stress Approach. *Journal of aging and health*, *31*(1), 37-66.

153. O'Neil, J. M. (2014). *Men's Gender Role Conflict*. Amer Psychological Assn.

154. *Ibid*

155. Stillson, R. W. (1988). Gender role conflict in adult men: A study of predictive variables. *Dissertation Abstracts International*, *50,366*.

156. Weiss, A. G. (2011). *Change Happens*. Rowman & Littlefield.

157. Freud, A. (1966). *The Ego and the Mechanisms of Defense*. International Universities Press Inc.

158. MacDonald, B. (2007). *Mrs. Piggle Wiggle*. Harper Collins.

159. Freud, A. (1966). *The Ego and the Mechanisms of Defense*. International Universities Press Inc

160. *Ibid*

161. Febos, M. (2011). *Whip Smart*. St. Martin's Griffin.

162. Cohen, R., Vedantam S. & Boyle T. (2018). Guys, We Have a Problem: How American Masculinity Creates Lonely Men. *Hidden Brain: A Conversation About Life's Unseen Patterns* https://www.npr.org/2018/03/19/594719471/guys-we-have-a-problem-how-american-masculinity-creates-lonely-men.

163. Joiner, T. (2011). *Lonely at the Top*. St. Martin's Press.

164. Baker, B. (03/09/17). The Biggest Threat Facing Middle Aged Men Isn't Smoking or Obesity. It's Loneliness. https://www.bostonglobe.com/magazine/2017/03/09/the-biggest-threat-facing-middle-age-men-isn-smoking-obesity-loneliness/k6saC9FnnHQCUbf5mJ8okL/story.html.

165. Joiner, T. (2011). *Lonely at the Top*. St. Martin's Press.

166. Mass General Hospital and Harvard Medical School. Harvard Study of Adult Development. https://www.adultdevelopmentstudy.org.

167. Mineo, L. (2017). Harvard study, almost 80 years old, has proved that embracing community helps us live longer, and be happier. Retrieved June 9, 2019, from https://news.harvard.edu/gazette/story/2017/04/over-nearly-80-years-harvard-study-has-been-showing-how-to-live-a-healthy-and-happy-life/.

168. Vadantam, S. (2018). Guys We Have a Problem: How American Masculinity Creates Lonely Men. *The Hidden Brain* https://www.npr.org/2018/03/19/594719471/guys-we-have-a-problem-how-american-masculinity-creates-lonely-men.

169. Holt-Lunstad, J., Smith, T. B., & Layton, J. B. (2010). Social relationships and mortality risk: a meta-analytic review. *PLoS medicine*, *7*, e1000316.

170. Hawkley, L. C., Thisted, R. A., Masi, C. M., & Cacioppo, J. T. (2010). Loneliness predicts increased blood pressure: 5-year cross-lagged analyses in middle-aged and older adults. *Psychology and aging*, *25*(1), 132.

171. House, J. S., Landis, K. R., & Umberson, D. (1988). Social relationships and health. *Science*, *241*(4865), 540-545.

172. Murphy, S. L., Xu, J., Kochanek, K. D., Curtin, S. C., & Arias, E. (2017). Deaths: final data for 2015. National Center for Biotechnology Information.

173. Schrodt, P., & Ledbetter, A. M. (2007). Communication processes that mediate family communication patterns and mental well-being: A mean and covariance structures analysis of young adults from divorced and nondivorced families. *Human Communication Research*, *33*(3), 330-356.

174. Stockett, K. (2009). *The Help [Hardcover]*. Amy Einhorn Books/Putnam.

175. Batrinos, M. L. (2012). Testosterone and aggressive behavior in man. *International journal of endocrinology and metabolism*, *10*(3), 563.

176. DiMuccio, S. H., & Knowles, E. D. (2020). The political significance of fragile masculinity. *Current Opinion in Behavioral Sciences*, *34*, 25-28.

177. O'Neil, J. M. (2014). *Men's Gender Role Conflict*. Amer Psychological Assn.

178. Vandello, J. A., Hettinger, V. E., Bosson, J. K., & Siddiqi, J. (2013). When equal isn't really equal: The masculine dilemma of seeking work flexibility. *Journal of Social Issues*, *69*(2), 303-321.

179. Hughes, J. (1987). Planes, Trains and Automobiles. Hughes Entertainment.

180. Ibid

181. Adams, H.E., Wright Hr., L. W., & Lohr, B.A. (1996). Is homophobia associated with homosexual arousal. *Journal of abnormal psychology*, *105*(3), 440.

182. Springer, K. W., & Mouzon, D. M. (2011). "Macho men" and preventive health care: Implications for older men in different social classes. *Journal of Health and Social Behavior*, *52*(2), 212-227.

183. Weiss, A. (2017). Men and Psychotherapy: What's in It for You? https://goodmenproject.com/featured-content/men-and-psychotherapy-whats-in-it-for-you-wcz/.

184. Yousaf, O., Popat, A., & Hunter, M. S. (2015). An investigation of masculinity attitudes, gender, and attitudes toward psychological help-seeking. *Psychology of Men & Masculinity*, *16*(2), 234.

185. Centers for Disease Control and Prevention. (04/13/17). Deaths: Final Data for 2014. *National Vital Statistics Report* https://www.cdc.gov/nchs/data/nvsr/nvsr65/nvsr65_04.pdf.

186. Mahalik, J. R., Burns, S. M., & Syzdek, M. (2007). Masculinity and perceived normative health behaviors as predictors of men's health behaviors. *Social science & medicine*, *64*(11), 2201-2209.

187. Wee, S.-L. (2018). In China, a School Trains Boys to be "Real Men.". *New York Times*.

188. Wilkerson, I. (2020). *Caste*. Penguin Random House.

189. Smith, S. G., Basile, K. C., Gilbert, L. K., Merrick, M. T., Patel, N., Walling, M. et al. (2017). National intimate partner and sexual violence survey (NISVS): 2010-2012 state report.

190. United Nations General Assembly (1993). Declarations on the elimination of violence towards women. *Proceedings of the 85th Plenary Meeting, Geneva.*

191. American Psychological Association (2/9/19). APA guidelines for psychological practice with boys and men. http://www.apa.org/about/policy/psychological-practice-boys-men-guidelines.pdg.

192. Cross, E. J., Overall, N. C., Low, R. S. T., & McNulty, J. K. (2018). An interdependence account of sexism and power: men's hostile sexism, biased perceptions of low power, and relationship aggression. *Journal of personality and social psychology*. 117, (2), 338-363.

193. Bugental, D. B. (2010). Paradoxical power manifestations: Power assertion by the subjectively powerless. Guilford.

194. Bugental, D. B., & Lin, E.K. (2001). The many faces of power: The strange case of Dr. Jekyll and Mr. Hyde. In A. Y. L.-C. J. A. Bargh (Ed.), *The use and abuse of power: Multiple perspectives on the causes of corruption* (pp. 115-132). New York: Psychology Press.

195. Overall, N., Hammond, M., McNulty, J., & Finkel, J. (2016). When power shapes interpersonal behavior:

Low relationship power predicts men's aggressive responses to low situational power. *Journal of Personality and Social Psychology*, 111 (2), 195.

196. Worchel, S., Arnold, S. E., & Harrison, W. (1978). Aggression and power restoration: The effects of identifiability and timing on aggressive behavior. *Journal of Experimental Social Psychology*, *14*(1), 43-52.

197. Cross, E. J., Overall, N. C., Low, R. S. T., & McNulty, J. K. (2018). An interdependence account of sexism and power: men's hostile sexism, biased perceptions of low power, and relationship aggression. *Journal of personality and social psychology*. 117, (2), 338-363.

198. Ducat, S. (2005). *The Wimp Factor: Gender Gaps, Holy Wars, and the Politics of Anxious Masculinity* (1st ed.). Beacon Press.

199. Beinart, P. (2016). Fear of a female president. *The Atlantic*, *15*.

200. *Ibid*

201. Willer, R., Rogalin, C. L., Conlon, B., & Wojnowicz, M. T. (2013). Overdoing gender: A test of the masculine overcompensation thesis. *American journal of sociology*, *118*(4), 980-1022.

202. Ducat, S. (2005). *The Wimp Factor: Gender Gaps, Holy Wars, and the Politics of Anxious Masculinity* (1st ed.). Beacon Press.

203. Krieg, G. (2016). Donald Trump defends the size of his penis. *Washington Post.*

204. Moraes, L. (2016). Donald Trump's testosterone level gets big applause on 'Dr. Oz" show. Retrieved December 1, 2018, from https://deadline.com/2016/09/donald-trump-testosterone-level-applause-dr-oz-show-1201820359/.

205. Baumeister, R. F., & Sommer, K. L. (1997). What do men want? Gender differences and two spheres of belongingness: Comment on Cross and Madson (1997).

206. Gallagher, B. J. (2012). Women's Sexuality and Men's Fears. Retrieved February 1, 2019, from https://www.huffingtonpost.com/bj-gallagher/womens-sexuality-and-mens_b_1289564.html.

207. Rosin, H. (2010). The end of men: How women are taking control of everything. https://www.theatlantic.com/magazine/archive/2010/07/the-end-of-men/308135/.

208. *Ibid*

209. *Ibid*

210. Deaton, A. C., A. (2017). Mortality and Morbidity in the 21st Century. https://www.brookings.edu/bpea-articles/mortality-and-morbidity-in-the-21st-century/.

211. Freud, S. (1937). *Analysis terminable and interminable* (22). London: Hogarth Press.

212. Ducat, S. (2005). *The Wimp Factor: Gender Gaps, Holy Wars, and the Politics of Anxious Masculinity* (1st ed.). Beacon Press.

213. Schwartz, B. J. (1955). The measurement of castration anxiety and anxiety over loss of love. *Journal of Personality*. 24,204-219.

214. Horney, K. (1932). Observations on a Specific Difference in the Dread Felt by Men and by Women Respectively for the Opposite Sex. *International Journal of Psychoanalysis*, *13*, 348-360.

215. Blazina, C. (1997). The fear of the feminine in the western psyche and the masculine task of disidentification: Their effect on the development of masculine gender role conflict. *The Journal of Men's Studies,* 6), 55-68.

216. Jones, E. (1956). *Sigmund Freud: life and work: vol.2: the years of maturity 1901-1919*. Basic Books.

217. Bowlby, J. (1969). Attachment and loss: volume I: attachment. London: The Hogarth Press and the Institute of Psycho-Analysis.

218. Ainsworth, M. D. S., Blehar, M. C., Waters, E., & Wall, S. N. (2015). *Patterns of Attachment*. Psychology Press.

219. Bowlby, J. (1969). Attachment and loss: volume I: attachment. London: The Hogarth Press and the Institute of Psycho-Analysis.

220. Gottman, J. (2018). *The Seven Principles for Making Marriage Work*. Seven Dials.

221. O'Neil, J. M. (2014). *Men's Gender Role Conflict*. Amer Psychological Assn.

222. Bakermans-Kranenburg, M. J., & van IJzendoorn, M. H. (2009). The first 10,000 Adult Attachment Interviews: Distributions of adult attachment representations in clinical and non-clinical groups. *Attachment & human development*, *11*(3), 223-263.

223. Jordan, J., Kaplan, A., Stiver, I., Surrey, J., Miller, J. (1991). *Women's growth in connection: Writings from the Stone Center*. Guilford ress.

224. Lachkar, J. (2004). *The Narcissistic / Borderline Couple*. Routledge.

225. Dinnerstein, D. (1999). *The Mermaid and the Minotaur*. New York: Other Books.

226. Ibid

227. Bartling, K., Kopp, F., & Lindenberger, U. (2010). Maternal affect attunement: Refinement and internal validation of a coding scheme. *International Journal of Developmental Science*, *4*(1), 1-17.

228. Tronick, E., Als, H., Adamson, L., Wise, S., & Brazelton, T. B. (1978). The infant's response to entrapment between contradictory messages in face-to-face interaction. *Journal of the American Academy of Child psychiatry*, *17*(1), 1-13.

229. Dinnerstein, D. (1999). *The Mermaid and the Minotaur*. New York: Other Books.

230. *Ibid*

231. Merriam-Webster. (2020). *Merriam-Webster's Dictionary and Thesaurus*. Merriam-Webster

232. Weiss, A. G. (2011). *Change Happens*. Rowman & Littlefield.

233. Kaufman, M. (1994). *Cracking the Armour*. Penguin.

234. Addis, M. E., & Mahalik, J. R. (2003). Men, masculinity, and the contexts of help seeking. *American psychologist*, *58*(1), 5.

235. O'Neil, J. M. (2014). *Men's Gender Role Conflict*. Amer Psychological Assn.

236. Lin, L., Stamm, K., & Christidis, P. (2018). Demographics of the US psychology workforce. *Washington, DC: American Psychological Association.*.

237. Joiner, T. (2011). *Lonely at the Top*. St. Martin's Press.

238. Dinnerstein, D. (1999). *The Mermaid and the Minotaur*. New York: Other Books.

239. Moore, D. S. (2015). *The Developing Genome*. Oxford University Press, USA.

240. Gottman, J. (2018). *The Seven Principles for Making Marriage Work*. Seven Dials.

241. Ibid

242. Jack, D. C. (1993). *Silencing The Self*. Harper Collins.

243. Felder, R. (1986). Anxiety is contagious.

244. Teutsch, D. A. (2006). *A Guide to Jewish Practice*. Wayne State University Press.

245. Joiner, T. (2011). *Lonely at the Top*. St. Martin's Press.

246. Gottman, J. (2018). *The Seven Principles for Making Marriage Work*. Seven Dials.

247. National Broadcasting Company. This is Us. https://www.nbc.com/this-is-us.

248. Tronick, E., Als, H., Adamson, L., Wise, S., & Brazelton, T. B. (1978). The infant's response to entrapment between contradictory messages in face-to-face interaction. *Journal of the American Academy of Child psychiatry*, *17*(1), 1-13.

Bibliography

Adams, R. (9/22/14). Study Finds that 'Happy Wife, Happy Life' is Pretty Dead On. Retrieved May 19, 2019, from https://www.huffpost.com/entry/happy-wife-happy-life_n_5843596.

Addis, M. E., & Mahalik, J. R. (2003). Men, masculinity, and the contexts of help seeking. *American psychologist*, *58*(1), 5.

Ainsworth, M. D. S., Blehar, M. C., Waters, E., & Wall, S. N. (2015). *Patterns of Attachment*. Psychology Press.

American Psychological Association, B. A. M. G. G. (2/9/19). APA guidelines for psychological practice with boys and men. http://www.apa.org/about/policy/psychological-practice-boys-men-guidelines.pdg.

Aneshensel, C. S., Frerichs, R. R., & Clark, V. A. (1981). Family roles and sex differences in depression. *Journal of Health and Social Behavior*, 379-393.

Appleby, D. W., & Palkovitz, R. (2007). Factors influencing a divorced father's involvement with his children.

Archer, J. (2000). Sex differences in aggression between heterosexual partners: A meta-analytic review. *Psychological bulletin*, *126*(5), 651.

Autor, D., Dorn, D., & Hanson, G. (2018). When work disappears: Manufacturing decline and the falling marriage-market value of young men. *American Economic Review: Insights*.

Baker, B. (03/09/17). The Biggest Threat Facing Middle Aged Men Isn't Smoking or Obesity. It's Loneliness. https://www.bostonglobe.com/magazine/2017/03/09/the-biggest-threat-facing-middle-age-men-isn-smoking-obesity-loneliness/k6saC9FnnHQCUbf5mJ8okL/story.html.

Bakermans-Kranenburg, M. J., & van IJzendoorn, M. H. (2009). The first 10,000 Adult Attachment Interviews: Distributions of adult attachment representations in clinical and non-clinical groups. *Attachment & human development*, *11*(3), 223-263.

Banaji, M. R., & Prentice, D. A. (1994). The self in social contexts. *Annual review of psychology*, *45*(1), 297-332.

Bareket, O., Kahalon, R., Shnabel, N., & Glick, P. (2018). The Madonna-Whore Dichotomy: Men who perceive women's nurturance and sexuality as mutually exclusive endorse patriarchy and show lower relationship satisfaction. *Sex Roles*, *79*(9), 519-532.

Barkhorn, E. (2013). Are successful women really less likable than successful men. *The Atlantic*.

Barry, R. A., & Lawrence, E. (2013). "Don't stand so close to me": An attachment perspective of disengagement and avoidance in marriage. *Journal of Family Psychology*, *27*(3), 484.

Bartling, K., Kopp, F., & Lindenberger, U. (2010). Maternal affect attunement: Refinement and internal validation of a coding scheme. *International Journal of Developmental Science*, *4*(1), 1-17.

Bates, E. A., Graham-Kevan, N., & Archer, J. (2014). Testing predictions from the male control theory of men's partner violence. *Aggressive behavior*, *40*(1), 42-55.

Baumeister, R. F., & Sommer, K. L. (1997). What do men want? Gender differences and two spheres of belongingness: Comment on Cross and Madson (1997).

Baumeister, R. F. (2010). *Is There Anything Good About Men.* Oxford University Press.

Bederman, G. *Manliness and Civilization: A Cultural History of Gender and Race in the United States. Chicago:Cited in Ducat, S. (1995) The Wimp Factor.* Chicagop: University of Chicago Press.

Beinart, P. (2016). Fear of a female president. *The Atlantic, 15.*

Blazina, C. (1997). The fear of the feminine in the western psyche and the masculine task of disidentification: Their effect on the development of masculine gender role conflict. *The Journal of Men's Studies,* 6), 55-68.

Borthick, M. J. (1998). Gender role conflict and suicidal ideation in an adolescent and young adult population: Age 18-24 years. *Dissertation Abstracts International*, *58*, 18-24.

Bowlby, J. (1969). Attachment and loss: volume I: attachment. In *Attachment and Loss: Volume I: Attachment* (pp. 1-

401). London: The Hogarth Press and the Institute of Psycho-Analysis.

Breiding, M. J., Windle, C. R., & Smith, D. A. (2008). Interspousal criticism: A behavioral mediator between husbands' gender role conflict and wives' adjustment. *Sex roles*, *59*(11-12), 880-888.

Bruce, L. (1975). *The Essential Lenny Bruce*. Harvill Press.

Bugental, D. B., & Lin, E.K. (2001). The many faces of power: The strange case of Dr. Jekyll and Mr. Hyde. In A. Y. L.-C. J. A. Bargh (Ed.), *The use and abuse of power: Multiple perspectives on the causes of corruption* (pp. 115-132). New York: Psychology Press.

Bugental, D. B. (2010). Paradoxical power manifestations: Power assertion by the subjectively powerless.

Burr, B. Retrieved September 17, 2017, from https://www.youtube.com/watch?list=RDspinaW-zC-E&v=kk5iqoYVUQc.

Butler, S. (1759). *The Geunuine Remains in Verse and Prose of Mr. Samuel Butler, Author of* Hudibras. (II). London: Toson, in the Strang.

Campbell, A. (1981). *The Sense of Well-Being in America: Recent Patterns and Trends*. New York: McGraw Hill.

Campbell, J. (1968). *Creative Mythology*. New York: Viking Press.

Caprino, K. Renowned threrapist explains the crushing eff.

Carnes, M. (1989). *Secret Ritual and Manhood in Victorian America. Cited in Ducat, S. The Wimp Factor*. New Haven, CT: Yale University Press.

Carr, D., Freedman, V. A., Cornman, J. C., & Schwarz, N. (2014). Happy marriage, happy life? Marital quality and subjective well-being in later life. *Journal of Marriage and Family*, *76*(5), 930-948.

Cashion, B. E. (1970). Durkheim's Concept of Anomie and It's Relationship to Divorce. *Sociology and Social Research*, *55*, 72-81.

Cassino, D. (2018). Emasculation, Conservatism, and the 2016 Election. *Contexts*, *17*(1), 48-53.

Celentana, M. A. (2000). Men's gender role adherence, relational partners psychological well-being, and constructivist measures of intimacy (Doctoral dissertation, Miami University, 2000). *Dissertation Abstracts International*, *61*, 5555.

Control, C. F. D. P. N. (2001). (2001), National Intimate Partner nad Sexual Violence Survey, United States.

Control, C. F. D. P. N. (2011). National Intimate Partner and Sexual Violence Survery. United States.

Chadwick, S. B., & van Anders, S. M. (2017). Do women's orgasms function as a masculinity achievement for men. *The Journal of sex research*, *54*(9), 1141-1152.

Chapman, G. (2014). *The 5 Love Languages for Men*. Moody Publishers.

Chen, Z., Fiske, S. T., & Lee, T. L. (2009). Ambivalent sexism and power-related gender-role ideology in marriage. *Sex roles*, *60*(11-12), 765-778.

Christensen, A. (1988). Dysfunctional interaction patterns in couples. In P. F. Noller, M.A. (Ed.), *Perspectives on martial interaction* (pp. 31-52).

Clover, C. J. (2015). *Men, Women, and Chain Saws: Gender in the Modern Horror Film-Updated Edition* (15). Princeton University Press.

Cohen, R., Vedantam S. & Boyle T. (2018). Guys, We Have a Problem: How American Masculinity Creates Lonely Men. *Hidden Brain: A Conversation About Life's Unseen Patterns* https://www.npr.org/2018/03/19/594719471/guys-we-have-a-problem-how-american-masculinity-creates-lonely-men.

Cohen, R. (2015). Welcome to the manosphere: A brief guide to the controversial men's rights movement. Retrieved April 6, 2019, from https://www.motherjones.com/politics/2015/01/manosphere-mens-rights-movement-terms/.

Collins, N. L., & Feeney, B. C. (2004). Working models of attachment shape perceptions of social support: evidence from experimental and observational studies. *Journal of personality and social psychology*, *87*(3), 363.

Coombs, R. H. (1991). Marital status and personal well-being: A literature review. *Family relations*, *40*(1), 97-102.

Corsini, R. (2016). *The Dictionary of Psychology*. Routledge.

Cross, E. J., Overall, N. C., Low, R. S. T., & McNulty, J. K. (2018). An interdependence account of sexism and power: men's hostile sexism, biased perceptions of low power, and relationship aggression. *Journal of personality and social psychology.*

Cross, S. E., & Madson, L. (1997). Models of the self: self-construals and gender. *Psychological bulletin, 122*(1), 5.

Csikszentmihalyi, M. (2013). *Creativity.* Harper Perennial.

Curtin, S. C., Warner, M. & Hedegaard, H. (2016). Suicide Rates for Females and Males by Race and Ethnicity: United States 1999 and 2014. https://www.cdc.gov/nchs/data/hestat/suicide/rates_1999_2014.pdf.

De Lange, J. (1980). Interpersonal Relations: A Theory of Interdependence. By Harold H. Kelley and John W. Thibaut. New York: John Wiley & Sons, 1978. 341 pp. $18.95.

DeAngelo, D. (03/25/21). Ten Most Dangerous Mistakes Men Make with Women. https://www.nairaland.com/89759/ten-most-dangerous-mistakes-men.

Deaton, A. C., A. (2017). Mortality and Morbidity in the 21st Century. https://www.brookings.edu/bpea-articles/mortality-and-morbidity-in-the-21st-century/.

Diamond, J. (2017). The one thing men want more than sex. *Good Men Project.*

DiMuccio, S. H., & Knowles, E. D. (2020). The political significance of fragile masculinity. *Current Opinion in Behavioral Sciences*, *34*, 25-28.

Dinnerstein, D. (1999). *The Mermaid and the Minotaur*. New York: Other Books.

Downey, G., & Feldman, S. I. (1996). Implications of rejection sensitivity for intimate relationships. *Journal of personality and social psychology*, *70*(6), 1327.

Ducat, S. (2005). *The Wimp Factor: Gender Gaps, Holy Wars, and the Politics of Anxious Masculinity* (1st ed.). Beacon Press.

Elam, P. (10/17/16). What Men Fear Most. https://avoiceformen.com/featured/what-men-fear-most/.

Erikson, E. H. (1994). *Identity: Youth and Crisis*. W. W. Norton & Company.

Faris, J. (2017). More than an Orgasm. https://avoiceformen.com/men/more-than-an-orgasm/.

Febos, M. (2011). *Whip Smart*. St. Martin's Griffin.

Felder, R. (1986). Anxiety is contagious.

Felder, R. E., & Weiss, A. G. (1991). *Experiential Psychotherapy*. University Press of Amer.

Fisher, T. D., Moore, Z. T., & Pittenger, M.-J. (2012). Sex on the brain?: An examination of frequency of sexual cognitions as a function of gender, erotophilia, and social desirability. *Journal of Sex Research*, *49*(1), 69-77.

Fiske, A. P., Haslam, N., & Fiske, S. T. (1991). Confusing one person with another: What errors reveal about the elementary forms of social relations. *Journal of personality and social psychology, 60*(5), 656.

Fogarty, T. F. (1976). Marital Crisis. In P. J. Guerin (Ed.), *Family Therapy: Theory and Practice* (pp. 325-334). New York: Gardner Press.

Freud, A. (1966). *The Ego and the Mechanisms of Defense.* International Universities PressInc.

Freud, S. (1937). *Analysis terminable and interminable* (22). London: Hogarth Press.

Freud, S. (1921). *The Interpretation of Dreams.*

Gallagher, B. J. (2012). Women's Sexuality and Men's Fears. Retrieved February 1, 2019, from https://www.huffingtonpost.com/bj-gallagher/womens-sexuality-and-mens_b_1289564.html.

Gennep, A. V. (2013). *The Rites of Passage.* Routledge.

Gilligan, C. (1977). In a different voice: Women's conceptions of self and of morality. *Harvard educational review, 47*(4), 481-517.

Glick, P., & Fiske, S. T. (1996). The ambivalent sexism inventory: Differentiating hostile and benevolent sexism. *Journal of personality and social psychology, 70*(3), 491.

Glick, P., Sakalli-Ugurlu, N., Ferreira, M. C., & Souza, M. A. D. (2002). Ambivalent sexism and attitudes toward wife abuse in Turkey and Brazil. *Psychology of Women Quarterly, 26*(4), 292-297.

Goodwin, P. (2009). *Who Marries and When?: Age at First Marriage in the United States, 2002* ((19)). US Department of Health and Human Services, Centers for Disease Control and ….

Gottman, J. (2018). *The Seven Principles for Making Marriage Work*. Seven Dials.

Gottman, J., & Silver, N. (2015). *The Seven Principles for Making Marriage Work*. Harmony.

Gottman, J. M., & Levenson, R. W. (1988). The social psychophysiology of marriage.

Gove, W. R., & Tudor, J. F. (1973). Adult sex roles and mental illness. *American journal of Sociology*, *78*(4), 812-835.

Graham, C. A., Mercer, C. H., Tanton, C., Jones, K. G., Johnson, A. M., Wellings, K. et al. (2017). What factors are associated with reporting lacking interest in sex and how do these vary by gender? Findings from the third British national survey of sexual attitudes and lifestyles. *BMJ open*, *7*(9).

Gray, J. (1993). *Men Are from Mars, Women Are from Venus*. Harper Collins.

Gurin, G., Veroff, J., & Feld, S. (1960). Americans view their mental health: A nationwide interview survey.

Guttentag, M., & Secord, P. F. (1983). *Too many women: The Sex Ration Question*. Sage Publications, Inc.

Hammond, M. D., & Overall, N. C. (2013). Men's hostile sexism and biased perceptions of intimate partners: Fostering dissatisfaction and negative behavior in close relationships. *Personality and Social Psychology Bulletin, 39*(12), 1585-1599.

Harris, M. (1999). *Cultural anthropology (3rd edition).* Allyn & Bacon.

Hawkley, L. C., Thisted, R. A., Masi, C. M., & Cacioppo, J. T. (2010). Loneliness predicts increased blood pressure: 5-year cross-lagged analyses in middle-aged and older adults. *Psychology and aging, 25*(1), 132.

Hayak, S. (2017). Harvey Weinstein Is My Monster Too. *New York Times.*

Hays, H. R. (1964). *The dangerous sex: The Myth of Feminie Evil.* New York: G.P. Putnam's Sons.

Herrera, M. C., Expósito, F., & Moya, M. (2012). Negative reactions of men to the loss of power in gender relations: Lilith vs. Eve. *The European Journal of Psychology Applied to Legal Context, 4*(1), 17.

Hill, D. B., & Menvielle, E. (2009). "You have to give them a place where they feel protected and safe and loved": The views of parents who have gender-variant children and adolescents. *Journal of LGBT Youth, 6*(2-3), 243-271.

Hogendoorn, B., Leopold, T., & Bol, T. (2020). Divorce and diverging poverty rates: A risk-and-vulnerability approach. *Journal of Marriage and Family, 82*(3), 1089-1109.

Holt-Lunstad, J., Smith, T. B., & Layton, J. B. (2010). Social relationships and mortality risk: a meta-analytic review. *PLoS medicine, 7*, e1000316.

Horney, K. (1932). Observations on a Specific Difference in the Dread Felt by Men and by Women Respectively for the Opposite Sex. *International Journal of Psychoanalysis*, *13*, 348-360.

Horsmon, S. 21 Things Unhappy Husbands are Afraid to Say Out Loud. Retrieved March 18, 2018, from https://goodmenproject.com/marriage-2/21-things-unhappy-husbands-are-afraid-to-say-out-loud-stvhn/.

House, J. S., Landis, K. R., & Umberson, D. (1988). Social relationships and health. *Science*, *241*(4865), 540-545.

Hughes, J. (1987). Planes, Trains and Automobiles.

Hymowitz, K. S. (2008). Love in the Time of Darwinism. *City Journal*, *18*(4).

Jack, D. C. (1993). *Silencing The Self*. Harper Collins.

Penny, J. C. (2009). Beware the Doghouse. https://www.youtube.com/watch?v=Twivg7GkYts.

Joiner, T. (2011). *Lonely at the Top*. St. Martin's Press.

Jones, E. (1956). *Sigmund Freud: life and work: vol.2: the years of maturity 1901-1919*.

Jones, M. (2/11/18). When Porn is Sex Ed.

Jordan, J., Kaplan, A., Stiver, I., Surrey, J., Miller, J. (1991). *Women's growth in connection: Writings from the Stone Center*. guilford press.

Jung, C. G. (2014). *The Archetypes and the Collective Unconscious*. Routledge.

Kasser, T. (2002). *The high Price of Materialism*. Cambridge, MA: MIT Press.

Kaufman, M. (1994). *Cracking the Armour*. Penguin.

Kawachi, I., Colditz, G. A., Ascherio, A., Rimm, E. B., Giovannucci, E., Stampfer, M. J. et al. (1996). A prospective study of social networks in relation to total mortality and cardiovascular disease in men in the USA. *Journal of Epidemiology & Community Health*, *50*(3), 245-251.

Keddie, A. (2003). Little boys: Tomorrow's macho lads. *Discourse: studies in the cultural politics of education*, *24*(3), 289-306.

Kelley, H. H., & Thibaut, J. W. (1978). *Interpersonal relations: A Theory of Interdependence*. New York: John Wiley & Sons.

Kierski, W., & Blazina, C. (2010). The male fear of the feminine and its effects on counseling and psychotherapy. *The Journal of Men's Studies*, *17*(2), 155-172.

Kim, C. The Gendered Landscape of Self-Silencing. Retrieved 2/3/19, https://steinhardt.nyu.edu/appsych/opus/issues/2015/fall/kim.

Kimmel, M. S. (2004). Masculinity as homophobia: Fear, shame, and silence in the construction of gender identity. *Race, class, and gender in the United States: An integrated study*, *81*, 93.

Klein, J. (2006). Cultural capital and high school bullies: How social inequality impacts school violence. *Men and Masculinities*, *9*(1), 53-75.

Knowles, E. D., S. (2018). How Donald Trump appeals to men secretly insecure about their manhood. *The Washington Post*.

Kobyashi. (1989).

Kosciw, J. G., Greytak, E. A., Bartkiewicz, M. J., Boesen, M. J., & Palmer, N. A. (2012). *The 2011 National School Climate Survey: The Experiences of Lesbian, Gay, Bisexual and Transgender Youth in Our Nation's Schools*. ERIC.

Krieg, G. (2016). Donald Trump defends the size of his penis. *Washington Post*.

Lachkar, J. (2004). *The Narcissistic / Borderline Couple*. Routledge.

Lachkar, J. (2004). *The Narcissistic / Borderline Couple*. Routledge.

Landau, M. J., Goldenberg, J. L., Greenberg, J., Gillath, O., Solomon, S., Cox, C. et al. (2006). The siren's call: Terror management and the threat of men's sexual attraction to women. *Journal of personality and social psychology*, *90*(1), 129.

Lea, H. C. (1961). *A History of the Inquisition of the Middle Ages*. New York: Macmillan.

Lederer, W. (1968). *The Fear of Women: An Inquiry Into the Enigma of Women and Why Men Through the Ages Have*

Both Loved and Dreaded Her. New York: Harcourt, Brace Jovanovich.

Levinson, D. J. (1978). *The Seasons of a Man's Life*. Random House Digital, Inc.

Levy, G. D., Taylor, M. G., & Gelman, S. A. (1995). Traditional and evaluative aspects of flexibility in gender roles, social conventions, moral rules, and physical laws. *Child development*, *66*(2), 515-531.

Ley, D. (2017). Why He Care About Your Orgasm: Research Sheds Light on Men's Motivations for Giving Pleasure. https://www.psychologytoday.com/us/blog/women-who-stray/201703/why-he-cares-about-your-orgasm.

Lin, L., Stamm, K., & Christidis, P. (2018). Demographics of the US psychology workforce. *Washington, DC: Author*.

Lockman, D. (2019). What 'Good' Dads Get Away With. Retrieved May 10, 2019, from https://www.nytimes.com/2019/05/04/opinion/sunday/men-parenting.html.

Maccoby, E. E. (1988). Gender as a social category. *Developmental Psychology*, *24*, 755-765.

MacDonald, B. (2007). *Mrs. Piggle Wiggle*. Harper Collins.

Mahalik, J. R., Aldarondo, E., Gilbert-Gokhale, S., & Shore, E. (2005). The role of insecure attachment and gender role stress in predicting controlling behaviors in men who batter. *Journal of Interpersonal Violence*, *20*(5), 617-631.

Mahalik, J. R., Burns, S. M., & Syzdek, M. (2007). Masculinity and perceived normative health behaviors as predictors of men's health behaviors. *Social science & medicine*, *64*(11), 2201-2209.

Mahalik, J. R., Good, G. E., Tager, D., Levant, R. F., & Mackowiak, C. (2012). Developing a taxonomy of helpful and harmful practices for clinical work with boys and men. *Journal of counseling psychology*, *59*(4), 591.

Margolin, G., Talovic, S., & Weinstein, C. D. (1983). Areas of Change Questionnaire: A practical approach to marital assessment. *Journal of Consulting and Clinical Psychology*, *51*(6), 920.

Marikar, S. (2018). Teachable Moment: He Said, She Said. *The New Yorker*, 21.

Hospital, M. G., & School, H. M. Harvard Study of Adult Development. https://www.adultdevelopmentstudy.org.

May, C. (2017). Are Women More Emotionally Expressive than Men? Retrieved June 9, 2019, from https://www.scientificamerican.com/article/are-women-more-emotionally-expressive-than-men/?redirect=1.

McDermott, R. C., & Lopez, F. G. (2013). College men's intimate partner violence attitudes: Contributions of adult attachment and gender role stress. *Journal of counseling psychology*, *60*(1), 127.

Melissa, D. (2003). Anger across the gender divide: researchers strive to understand how men and women experience and express anger. *Monit Psychol*, *34*(3), 52.

Merriam-Webster. (2020). *Merriam-Webster's Dictionary and Thesaurus*. Merriam-Webster.

Messner, M. A. (1998). The Limits of "The Male Sex Role" An Analysis of the Men's Liberation and Men's Rights Movements' Discourse. *Gender & Society*, *12*(3), 255-276.

Mikulincer, M., & Shaver, P. R. (2003). The attachment behavioral system in adulthood: Activation, psychodynamics, and interpersonal processes. *Advances in experimental social psychology*, *35*, 56-152.

Miller, A. (1997). *The Drama of the Gifted Child*. Basic Books.

Mineo, L. (2017). Harvard study, almost 80 years old, has proved that embracing community helps us live longer, and be happier. Retrieved June 9, 2019, from https://news.harvard.edu/gazette/story/2017/04/over-nearly-80-years-harvard-study-has-been-showing-how-to-live-a-healthy-and-happy-life/.

Moore, D. S. (2015). *The Developing Genome*. Oxford University Press, USA.

Moraes, L. (2016). Donald Trump's testosterone level gets big applause on 'Dr. Oz" show. Retrieved December 1, 2018, from https://deadline.com/2016/09/donald-trump-testosterone-level-applause-dr-oz-show-1201820359/.

Morris, D. (1968). *The Naked Ape: A Zoologist'study of the Human Animal*. Cape.

Murphy, S. L., Xu, J., Kochanek, K. D., Curtin, S. C., & Arias, E. (2017). Deaths: final data for 2015.

(2002). My Big Fat Greek Wedding. https://www.youtube.com/watch?v=8fJoPI-xytM.

Company, N. B. This is Us. https://www.nbc.com/this-is-us.

Hotline, N. D. V. 50 Obstacles to Leaving: 1-10. Retrieved March 31, 2019, from https://www.thehotline.org/2013/06/10/50-obstacles-to-leaving-1-10/.

Radio, N. P. When the "White Tears" Just Keep Coming. Retrieved November 28, 2018, from https://www.npr.org/sections/codeswitch/2018/11/28/649537891/when-the-white-tears-just-keep-coming.

Neukrug, E. S. (2015). *The Sage encyclopedia of theory in counseling and psychotherapy*. SAGE Publications.

O'Neil, J. M. (2014). *Men's Gender Role Conflict*. Amer Psychological Assn.

Ogas, O., & Gaddam, S. (2011). *A billion wicked thoughts: What the world's largest experiment reveals about human desire.* Dutton/Penguin Books.

Oluo, I. (10/14/16). Men, You Can Survive Without Us - Please Try. https://theestablishment.co/men-you-can-survive-without-us-please-try-19352ada1b05/.

Overall, N. C., Hammond, M. D., McNulty, J. K., & Finkel, E. J. (2016). When power shapes interpersonal behavior: Low relationship power predicts men's aggressive responses to low situational power. *Journal of personality and social psychology*, *111*(2), 195.

Overall, N. C., Sibley, C. G., & Tan, R. (2011). The costs and benefits of sexism: Resistance to influence during relationship conflict. *Journal of Personality and Social Psychology*, *101*(2), 271.

Perel, E. (2007). *Mating in Captivity*. Harper Collins.

Piaget, J., & Inhelder, B. (2008). *The Psychology Of The Child.*

Pollack, W. S. (1995). *No man is an island: Toward a new psychoanalytic psychology of men.* Basic Books.

Pollak, S., & Gilligan, C. (1982). Images of violence in Thematic Apperception Test stories. *Journal of Personality and Social psychology*, *42*(1), 159.

Poulin, F., & Pedersen, S. (2007). Developmental changes in gender composition of friendship networks in adolescent girls and boys. *Developmental psychology*, *43*(6), 1484.

Networker, P. F. (2018). Esther Perel on the Paradox of Masculinity. Retrieved April 13, 2019, from https://www.psychotherapynetworker.org/blog/details/1555/esther-perel-on-the-paradox-of-masculinity.

Radloff, L. (1975). Sex differences in depression: The Effects of Occupation on Marital Status. *Sex roles*, *1*(3), 249-265.

Remes, O., Brayne, C., Van Der Linde, R., & Lafortune, L. (2016). A systematic review of reviews on the prevalence of anxiety disorders in adult populations. *Brain and behavior*, *6*(7), e00497.

Rivers, C., & Ph.D., R. B. (2013). *The Truth About Girls and Boys: Challenging Toxic Stereotypes About Our Children* (Reprint ed.). Columbia University Press.

Rochlen, A. B., & Mahalik, J. R. (2004). Women's Perceptions of Male Partners' Gender Role Conflict as Predictors of Psychological Well-Being and Relationship Satisfaction. *Psychology of Men & Masculinity*, *5*(2), 147.

Rotundo, A. *American Manhood: Transformations in Masculinity From the Revolution to the Modern Era. Cited in Ducat, S. 1995*. New York.: Basic Books.

Sakall, N. (2001). Beliefs about wife beating among Turkish college students: The effects of patriarchy, sexism, and sex differences. *Sex roles*, *44*(9-10), 599-610.

Schrodt, P., & Ledbetter, A. M. (2007). Communication processes that mediate family communication patterns and mental well-being: A mean and covariance structures analysis of young adults from divorced and nondivorced families. *Human Communication Research*, *33*(3), 330-356.

Schwartz, B. J. (1955). The measurement of castration anxiety and anxiety over loss of love. *Journal of Personality*.

Shakespeare, W. (2001). *Hamlet*. Classic Books Company.

Sharp, E. (2/22/21).

Shpancer, N. (2015). Is Marriage Worth the Trouble for Women? The Benefits Go Mostly to Men. Retrieved March 12, 2017, from https://www.psychologytoday.com/us/blog/insight-therapy/201510/is-marriage-worth-the-trouble-women.

Shutts, K., Kenward, B., Falk, H., Ivegran, A., & Fawcett, C. (2017). Early preschool environments and gender: Effects of gender pedagogy in Sweden. *Journal of experimental child psychology*, *162*, 1-17.

Smith, B. (2019). 10 Signs You're Whipped. Retrieved April 26, 2019, from https://www.mensfitness.com/women/dating-advice/10-signs-youre-whipped.

Smith, S. G., Basile, K. C., Gilbert, L. K., Merrick, M. T., Patel, N., Walling, M. et al. (2017). National intimate partner and sexual violence survey (NISVS): 2010-2012 state report.

Springer, K. W., Lee, C., & Carr, D. (2019). Spousal Breadwinning Across 30 Years of Marriage and Husbands' Health: A Gendered Life Course Stress Approach. *Journal of aging and health*, *31*(1), 37-66.

Springer, K. W., & Mouzon, D. M. (2011). "Macho men" and preventive health care: Implications for older men in different social classes. *Journal of Health and Social Behavior*, *52*(2), 212-227.

Springer, K. W., & Mouzon, D. M. (2011). "Macho men" and preventive health care: Implications for older men in different social classes. *Journal of Health and Social Behavior*, *52*(2), 212-227.

Stillson, R. W. (1988). Gender role conflict in adult men: A study of predictive variables. *Dissertation Abstracts International*, *50,366.*

Stiver, I. (1991). The Meanings of "Dependency" in female-male relationships. In Jordan, J., Kaplan, A., Stiver, I. (Ed.), *Women's Growth in Connection: Writings from the Stone Center*. New York: Guilford.

Stockett, K. (2009). *The Help [Hardcover]*. Amy Einhorn Books/Putnam.

Teutsch, D. A. (2006). *A Guide to Jewish Practice*. Wayne State University Press.

Thompson, J. M., Whiffen, V. E., & Aube, J. A. (2001). Does self-silencing link perceptions of care from parents and partners with depressive symptoms. *Journal of Social and Personal Relationships*, *18*(4), 503-516.

Trevor-Roper, H. R. (1965). *The Persecution of witches.* New York: American Heritage Publishing Company.

Tronick, E., Als, H., Adamson, L., Wise, S., & Brazelton, T. B. (1978). The infant's response to entrapment between contradictory messages in face-to-face interaction. *Journal of the American Academy of Child psychiatry*, *17*(1), 1-13.

U.S. Department of Labor, B. O. L. S. (4/20/17). Employment Characteristics of Families-2016. Retrieved February 12, 2018, from https://www.bls.gov/news.release/pdf/famee.pdf.

Assembly, U. N. G. (1993). Declarations on the elimination of violence towards women. *Proceedings of the 85th Plenary Meeting, Geneva.*

Vadantam, S. (2018). Guys We Have a Problem: How American Masculinity Creates Lonely Men. *The Hidden Brain* https://www.npr.org/2018/03/19/594719471/guys-we-have-a-problem-how-american-masculinity-creates-lonely-men.

Vandello, J. A., Hettinger, V. E., Bosson, J. K., & Siddiqi, J. (2013). When equal isn't really equal: The masculine dilemma of seeking work flexibility. *Journal of Social Issues*, *69*(2), 303-321.

Warkentin, J. (1956). Support through non-reassurance. *American journal of psychotherapy*, *10*(4), 709-715.

Way, N. (2011). *Deep secrets: Boy's friendships and the crisis of connection*. Cambridge, MA: Harvard university Press.

Wee, S.-L. (2018). In China, a School Trains Boys to be "Real Men.". *New York Times*.

Weinberg, M. K., Tronick, E. Z., Cohn, J. F., & Olson, K. L. (1999). Gender differences in emotional expressivity and self-regulation during early infancy. *Developmental psychology*, *35*(1), 175.

Weiss, A. (2015). Experiential Psychotherapy. In E. Neukrug (Ed.), *The Sage Encyclopedia of Theory in Counseling and Psychotherapy*. Sage.

Weiss, A. (2017). Men and Psychotherapy: What's in It for You? https://goodmenproject.com/featured-content/men-and-psychotherapy-whats-in-it-for-you-wcz/.

Weiss, A. G. (2018). What if He Can't? What if She Doesn't? *From Fear to Intimacy* https://goodmenproject.com/featured-content/what-if-i-cant-what-if-she-doesnt-wcz/.

Weiss, A. G. (2019). Men's Panic at the Thought Their Wives Might Stop "Helping" Them: Learning from Women how to be More Loving and Generous. https://goodmenproject.com/featured-content/mens-panic-at-the-thought-their-wives-might-stop-helping-them-wcz/.

Weiss, A. G. (2018). Men's Fears of Being Dominated and Controlled by Women. https://goodmenproject.com/featured-content/mens-fears-dominated-controlled-women-wcz/.

Weiss, A. G. (2021). *Living and Loving Mutually: How to Break Free from Hurtful Relationship Patterns*. Lasting Impact Press.

Weiss, A. G. (2019). Stop Apologizing If You Want to Improve Your Relationships. https://goodmenproject.com/featured-content/stop-apologizing-wcz/.

Weiss, A. G. (9/16/18). Why Men Think Women are Too Needy: Could it Be Becasue Men are Taught Not to Need Anything from Anyone? https://goodmenproject.com/featured-content/why-men-think-women-are-too-needy-wcz/.

Weiss, A. G. (2019). But I Am Listening to You: Right? *From Fear to Intimacy* https://www.psychologytoday.com/us/blog/fear-intimacy/201904/i-am-listening-you.

Weiss, A. G. (2019). Why Does Conflict Escalate Between Men and Women. *From Fear to Intimacy* https://www.psychologytoday.com/us/blog/fear-intimacy/201907/why-does-conflict-escalate-between-men-and-women.

Weiss, A. G. (2018). One Bit is All it Takes: What Men Can Learn From Rabbits About Relationships.

Weiss, A. G. (2018). Men's Anger Might Mask Fear: I Know You're Mad but You Might Also be Scared. *From Fear to Intimacy* https://www.psychologytoday.com/us/blog/fear-intimacy/201809/mens-anger-might-mask-fear.

Weiss, A. G. (2020). Who Gets Up in the Middle of the Night in Your House? Power Struggles Between Men and Women About Anxiety. https://www.psychologytoday.com/us/blog/fear-intimacy/202009/who-gets-in-the-middle-the-night-in-your-house.

Weiss, A. (2018). Can Men Talk About Our Pain? Without Subtly Asserting the Privilege of "White Tears?". Retrieved March 31, 2019, from https://goodmenproject.com/ethics-values/can-men-talk-about-our-pain-wcz/.

Weiss, A. G. (1986). *The patient's experience of privacy in psychotherapy.* Georgia State University.

Weiss, A. G. (2002). The lost role of dependency in psychotherapy. *Gestalt Review*, *6*(1), 6-17.

Weiss, A. G. (2011). *Change Happens*. Rowman & Littlefield.

Weisss, A. G. (9/26/20). Who Gets Up in the Middle of the Night in Your House? Power Struggles Between Men and Women about Anxiety. *Men's Fears of Women* https://www.psychologytoday.com/us/blog/fear-intimacy/202009/who-gets-in-the-middle-the-night-in-your-house.

Wester, S. R., Vogel, D. L., Pressly, P. K., & Heesacker, M. (2002). Sex differences in emotion: A critical review of the literature and implications for counseling psychology. *The Counseling Psychologist*, *30*(4), 630-652.

Wiesner, M. (1993). *Women and Gender in Early Modern Europe*. Cambridge, England: Cambridge University Press.

Wilkerson, I. (2020). *Caste*. Penguin Random House.

Willer, R., Rogalin, C. L., Conlon, B., & Wojnowicz, M. T. (2013). Overdoing gender: A test of the masculine overcompensation thesis. *American journal of sociology*, *118*(4), 980-1022.

Worchel, S., Arnold, S. E., & Harrison, W. (1978). Aggression and power restoration: The effects of identifiability and timing on aggressive behavior. *Journal of Experimental Social Psychology*, *14*(1), 43-52.

Yamawaki, N., Ostenson, J., & Brown, C.R. (2009). The functions of gender role traditionality, ambivalent sexism, injury, and frequency of assault on domestic violence perception: A study between Japanese and American college students. *Violence Against Women*, *15*, 1126-1142.

Yousaf, O., Popat, A., & Hunter, M. S. (2015). An investigation of masculinity attitudes, gender, and attitudes toward psychological help-seeking. *Psychology of Men & Masculinity*, *16*(2), 234.

Zinczenko, D., & Spiker, T. (2007). *Men, Love & Sex*. Rodale.

About the Author

Avrum G. Weis, Ph.D. is a clinical psychologist who sees individuals and couples for psychotherapy online. Dr. Weiss is recognized nationally for his pioneering work on the process of change in individuals and organizations.

Published Books

- *Change Happens: When to Try Harder and When to Stop Trying So Hard*, Rowman & Littlefield Publishers (November 3, 2011) http://bit.ly/AvrumWeissChangeHappens
- *Living and Loving Mutually: How To Break Free From Hurtful Relationship Patterns,* Lasting Impact Press, an imprint of Connection Victory Publishing Company (November 2020) https://www.amazon.com/Living-Loving-Mutually-Relationship-Patterns/dp/1643810316/
- *Hidden in Plain Sight: How Men's Fears of Women Shape Their Intimate Relationships,* Lasting Impact Press, an imprint of Connection Victory Publishing Company (September 2021) https://www.amazon.com/Hidden-Plain-Sight-Intimate-Relationships-ebook/dp/B09DTNR6ZC/

Articles/Columns by Avrum G. Weiss, Ph.D.

- Psychology Today: https://www.psychologytoday.com/us/therapists/avrum-geurin-weiss-atlanta-ga/42420
- The Good Men Project: https://goodmenproject.com/author/agweiss/

Connect With the Author

- Facebook: Page https://www.FB.com/AvrumWeissAuthor/
- Facebook Group: https://bit.ly/MensFearsOfWomenAvrumWeissFBGroup
- Landing page: https://bit.ly/AvrumWeissBooks
- Twitter: https://twitter.com/avrum_weiss
- To book a guest lecture or other speaking engagement: inforequest@connectionvictory.com
- Dr. Avrum Weiss' email address: <agweiss@comcast.net>

License and Foreign Rights

For information on obtaining a license to use this content, contact the publisher: <inforequest@connectionvictory.com>.

Also Published by Lasting Impact Press an Imprint of Connection Victory Publishing Company

Listed in order of first publication date.

- *How to Cope, Manage the Household, and Make Love When Your Wife Has Cancer: Practical Guidance for the Husband-Caregiver* by Michael D. Stalter, January 2016
- *Curbing Human Trafficking: Sex slavery is a horrific international crime against women, men, and children. You can help stop it.* by Mark J. Vruno, December 2017
- *A Broken System: Family Court in The United States, Volume 1* by Stephen Louis Krasner, February 2018
- *Man Box: Poems* by Cameron Conaway, April 2018
- *Love 5.0: The Secrets for Being Close Yet Free and Having a Marriage That Lasts Forever* by Jed Diamond, Ph.D., April 2018

- *How Did You Get Him To Eat That? 12 Parenting Practices That Lead to Healthy Eating* by John D Rich, Ph.D., June 2018
- *My Distant Dad: Healing the Family Father Wound* by Jed Diamond, Ph.D., June 2018
- *Healing the Family Father Wound: Your Playbook for Personal and Relationship Success*, by Jed Diamond, Ph.D. August 2018
- *A Broken System: Family Court in The United States, Volume 2* by Stephen Louis Krasner, September 2018
- *Positive Parenting: A Practical and Sometimes Humorous Approach To Applying The Research In Your Home With Gender Inclusivity*, Mutual Respect, and Empathy – and NO Spanking! By John D Rich, Ph.D., February 2019
- *Practical Parenting: A Workbook To Accompany Positive Parenting* by John D Rich, Ph.D.
- *tumbling: poetic thoughts from an anxious mind by* Elizabeth Joyce, November 2019
- *The Resilient WriterWheels: Can't Is A Bad Word* by Erin M. Kelly, May 2020
- *Living and Loving Mutually:How To Break Free From Hurtful Relationship Patterns* by Avrum G. Weiss, Ph.D. November 2020
- *Talkin' to You, Bro: Liberating Yourself From the Confusing and Ambiguous Messages of Contemporary Masculinity* by Elwood David Watson, Ph.D.,, September 21, 2021

- Hidden in Plain Sight: How Men's Fears of Women Shape Their Intimate Relationships by Avrum G. Weiss, Ph.D., September 2021

Coming Soon from Lasting Impact Press, an Imprint of Connection Victory Publishing Company

*Mick & Me: My Unlikely Friendship With Wrestling Legend Mick Foley*_by Erin M. Kelly, Fall 2021

Printed in Great Britain
by Amazon

19782853R00169